THE
MURDER
BUSINESS

THE
MURDER
BUSINESS

HOW THE MEDIA TURNS
CRIME INTO ENTERTAINMENT
AND SUBVERTS JUSTICE

BY MARK FUHRMAN

Since 1947
REGNERY
PUBLISHING, INC.
An Eagle Publishing Company • Washington, DC

Library of Congress Cataloging-in-Publication Data

Fuhrman, Mark.
  The murder business : how the media turns crime into entertainment and subverts justice / by Mark Fuhrman.
     p. cm.
  ISBN 978-1-59698-584-1
  1. Mass media and crime--United States. 2. Mass media and criminal justice--United States. 3. Murder in mass media--United States. 4. Mass media--Objectivity--United States. I. Title.
  P96.C742U635 2009
  364.152'340973--dc22
                           2009035322

Published in the United States by
Regnery Publishing, Inc.
One Massachusetts Avenue, NW
Washington, DC 20001
www.regnery.com

Manufactured in the United States of America

10 9 8 7 6 5 4 3 2 1

Books are available in quantity for promotional or premium use. Write to Director of Special Sales, Regnery Publishing, Inc., One Massachusetts Avenue NW, Washington, DC 20001, for information on discounts and terms or call (202) 216-0600.

Distributed to the trade by:
Perseus Distribution
387 Park Avenue South
New York, NY 10016

"In seeking truth you have to get both sides of the story."

—*Walter Cronkite*

CONTENTS

PROLOGUE

AT ANY GIVEN TIME, there are about 100,000 missing persons in the United States. About 80 percent of them are found alive. The rest are not. A small number of these cases explode into national obsessions as a mass media feeding frenzy ensues over their stories. Typically, the victims are female. Without exception, they are white and very pretty. In a ghoulish moment, American Murder meets *American Idol*, as America chooses its prettiest corpse, onto whom our collective horror is projected. It begins with a photograph that quickly becomes iconic in our culture, a name we adopt into our national conversation as if we were speaking of someone we all knew. JonBenét. Caylee. Stacy Peterson. Laci Peterson.

The media want stories to acquire "legs," but the right elements have to be present for it to happen. Even if the suspect is famous, it doesn't guarantee our full attention. In post-O. J. Simpson trial America, in times of economic instability, the sordid truth is that the perfect murder victim generates a lot of money. It creates its own industry that springs up, like a traveling carnival or freak show, in American living rooms. It sells dread to people safe behind locked doors, who hang on every "update," needing to believe that following each case and focusing on each detail can make their own communities safe from evil. No detail is too petty, as the story is combed for players, who quickly acquire a status, a mask, and a persona of either good or evil. The suspect fuels the frenzy; the unanswered questions keep it alive, driving up ratings and feeding the media.

It is the suspect who gets the ball into the air and keeps it there. Nobody ever got that ball aloft like O. J. Simpson in 1994—and the media never got over its desire to re-create the scope, length, and depth of that sensational trial. They all want the next O. J.

You could abolish famine in several third world countries with the money generated by one O. J. Simpson trial or, for that matter, one Caylee Anthony story. Considering the power and size of today's mass media, publishing industry, entertainment industry, and memorabilia markets, you literally cannot tabulate the colossal earnings of a single perfect murder—one that "has everything."

In this climate of increasingly breathless, sensationalized murder cases, stoked, fed, hyped, and marketed by the television media, the system set in place to investigate and prosecute crimes stands increasingly helpless in the storm. Against the seductions of mass media, tedious, detail-oriented, sober law enforcement—cops, detectives, judges—cannot compete. More often than not, the media beast takes the crime and runs away with it, obstructing and desecrating the case itself. Those in the media have bought off potential informants, made investigations nearly impossible to conduct, compromised witnesses, tipped off the defense about prosecution strategies, and made it nearly impossible for an impartial jury to be composed, because anybody with a TV set already has their mind made up.

Even as I write this, the media machine is cranking into overdrive disseminating Michael Jackson's death being classified as a homicide. They've spent weeks obsessively reporting on his memorial concert, career, custody battles over his children, and family squabbles—really, anything "Michael Jackson" that will prolong public interest. (To his family's dismay, even his recent internment was disrupted by media helicopters.) And though his physician has yet to be charged of a crime by police, the subsequent media spotlight has left Dr. Murray afraid to return calls or emails—even to supporters, as he explained in a video to the public, as he waits for the circus to end. Media attention should never get in the way of an active investigation—yet these detectives' every move is broadcast for the world to follow, which could easily harm their efforts to gather evidence and talk to witnesses.

———

Media and law enforcement all too frequently work at cross-purposes because they have different goals. Law enforcement wants to solve a case as fast as possible and put the guilty behind bars. The media want a case to drag on as long as humanly possible, and do all they can to extricate every last bit of drama, drop by bloody drop, in order to hold the attention of the millions of viewers who have gotten hooked. Law enforcement must abide by rules. The media make their own rules, and even then break them, or find ways to work loopholes into them. All that matters is ratings.

If people knew how it's done—how the media seduce, buy, bribe, and corrupt, like an inevitable, malignant cancer on a murder investigation—they might be too sickened to buy the next ticket to the carnival.

I am a detective but have crossed over into media, as a commentator and criminal investigator for FOX News, in the wake of my notorious role in the O. J. Simpson murder trial.

I hesitate to describe my experiences in that case. Everything that I remember, when placed on paper or spoken out loud, seems like whining or a plea for sympathy. I have been the target and subject of the media, been a cop for twenty years, been involved in the highest-profile case to date, and now I work for the media. Perhaps my experience can help change the way the media report murder.

The unfortunate truth is that today, each murder has many victims, and high-profile murders can hurt innocent people who get burned by the spotlight, whether or not they sought it out themselves. I learned that firsthand as a police witness in the O. J. Simpson trial, a wrenching experience that showed how the criminal justice system can be manipulated by money, power, politics, and fame. I have never revealed the full inside story of that case—the shocking missing chapters of history which only a few knew about—until today. Though I had seen a lot of darkness in the hearts of men over my career as a homicide detective, I was completely unprepared for the lengths the media went in pursuit of "the story," and the betrayals I experienced as people jumped out of the way of the media machine.

However, the Simpson trial came to serve as a template for high-profile cases, when it should have been seen as a model to be avoided.

Following the Simpson trial, I have covered almost every major murder case as a journalist, writing books and magazine articles, and providing commentary and analysis on television news programs.

Now I work exclusively for FOX News, which gives me the freedom and the resources to investigate cases almost the way I did as an LAPD detective. This second career is challenging and fascinating. I am grateful for the opportunity to continue my detective work as a private citizen. Yet it is not without its frustrations.

Even though I now work as a journalist, at heart I'm still a cop. This gives me a unique perspective on high-profile murder cases. I try to balance the often-conflicting responsibilities of truth, justice, and the public's right to know. For me, the greater good of helping law enforcement solve a case outweighs any other considerations. Every day I walk a line between my journalistic responsibilities and my desire to see justice done. It isn't always easy, but it's the only way I could do this job and sleep at night.

When I investigate a high-profile case as a reporter, I share information with the police. If I learn something that might harm the investigation, I won't reveal it (unless it involves misconduct or criminality on the part of the investigators). Often, I ask the police whether or not I can release information, knowing that they frequently need to hold back certain facts from public knowledge. Sometimes, I don't even have to ask—I already know what I should or shouldn't say. My highest priority is to help solve the case—not scoop the competition.

The truth about most of the media is probably unsurprising to anybody who has ever experienced how most reporters and TV hosts work. First of all, they don't actually investigate. They don't seek, hunt, explore, or solve crimes. Detectives do. In today's media climate, it is rare to have a journalist or network investigate material before it goes on the air. FOX is different—that why I work for them. FOX hires me, a former detective, to use my investigative skills to improve the quality of what they report, because the unfortunate truth is that all too often, the most common threat and block to law enforcement's capacity to do its job is not the suspect or the suspect's attorneys; it is the media. Many "reporters" stop at nothing; they have no code of conduct, no governing ethics, and no limit to their bribes. But again, what they want is the opposite of what we want. We want to solve the crime. They want to make a very lengthy spectacle out of it, and deliberately drag it out for months or even years after the truth and facts about the crime are already settled. It's the greatest show on earth in today's United States: Murder.

The underbelly of America is the lifeblood of the media—the thing it sells back to its audience. Depravity. Sociopathology. Amorality.

One myth is that the "news media" do not pay sources for information. They used to rely primarily on "wining and dining"—flying family members of victims to New York, putting them up in five-star hotels, springing for lavish restaurant meals, and maybe even purchasing theater tickets.

But in recent years, even that blurred line has been flagrantly crossed. Assuring themselves that "licensing" products is not the same as paying people outright, the media has been shelling out huge sums of money for the "use" of photographs, videotapes, personal items, and so forth. In other words, the family members and witnesses are paid for items as if they were media "content," which they also are, or become, when broadcast. But the cynical part is that functionally, they're offering bribes, baiting people, cementing loyalties, and fueling addictions. They don't outright pay for the interview, but that distinction is immaterial.

Let me give you an example. Roy Kronk, the meter-reader who came upon the remains of Caylee Anthony while urinating in a wooded area, was in the process of being flown to New York to appear on *Good Morning America*, by the ABC field producer at the time, my friend Steph Watts. He was not offering money, but certainly a lavish trip to New York. Suddenly he was told by an executive producer with ABC, "He's already booked. He's on the show tomorrow." Steph learned that *Good Morning America* had cut a check for $20,000 directly to the man, supposedly for the use of a photograph he took with his cell phone of the wooded area where he'd found the remains. Clearly, that photograph was not worth $20,000. But the network got days out of the "story" of the man's horrific discovery.

Where will it end? How ghoulish will the American people become? How far are we from people reaching for their cameras when they see crime, instead of their cell phones to call 911?

In the case of Caylee Anthony, a murder that has generated untold millions of dollars all around, we see an increasingly familiar story behind the screens. The child's grandparents were approached by a public relations figure, who persuaded them they needed "representation" to deal with the media. The PR rep then started negotiating and setting up bidding wars between the networks. He makes money, the family makes money, and the attorneys on the case earn name recognition, which translates into money.

The police, meanwhile, have their hands tied. Police do have an option of paying for certain types of information—but it must serve the goal of solving the crime—not creating drama aimed at generating ratings and prolonging a story at the risk of derailing justice. Police can offer an informant money only if the informant has given the police a lead that pans out and helps solve the crime. The networks, by contrast, gild the lily first—soaking families in goodies before they have given the interview. By the time they are on camera, they are like performing seals. They know they had better be good— give something juicy and make the audience gasp, in order to get more fish from the trainers.

Sometimes, rarely, the spotlight illuminates. Far more often, it blinds.

———————————

There was a time when more journalists were dedicated to reporting just the facts. Yet over the last decade, especially in broadcast news, facts have mostly been replaced with opinion, conversation, debate, and argument. News programs have become chat shows, complete with guests and even commentary from viewers. With so many opinions and so few facts, viewers are free to choose whichever opinions they favor.

But investigating a murder is not about opinion and debate. It shouldn't be reported in a newsy version of *The View*. Victims are real people. There are facts to be determined and reported. It's not just talk.

Detectives have the responsibility to see the one small, overlooked item, hear a voice inflection, or question the sobbing reenactment of the death of a loved one. Detectives are nice to their kids, dogs, and family, but view the rest of the world with a calculated scowl. We see the planet differently than most people. Darker, you might say.

There is no good detective who can tell you exactly how he untangles a crime. The process is as personal as one's inner thoughts. The irony is that there is no clear-cut process. Sure, there are predictable approaches to a crime scene, collection of evidence, and the "rules," but the real solutions come from another place. Good detectives have the ability to project themselves into the crime scene—into the victims' world and the actions of the suspect.

Life experience is not enough. Training is not sufficient. The essence of detectives' work is their ability to interact with an environment of chaos, danger, lies, and filth while making sense of it all. No police academy or university or law school can replicate the experience or the education. Yet now, as never before, everyone is an armchair sleuth while watching the cable and satellite networks that have made a cottage industry of murder.

In this book I will examine a series of high-profile cases, recounting the stories that have fascinated millions of people, but also reveal what went on behind the scenes. My television commentary is often the result of days, even weeks of investigation, much of which I don't publicly discuss. Now that many of these cases are closed, I can talk more candidly about my involvement in them. And during my investigations, I have seen how other members of the Murder Business conduct themselves. In twenty years of police work, I thought that the guilt or innocence of the suspect was all-important. Then I started covering high-profile murder cases, where ratings and profit often far outweigh the importance of facts.

The Murder Business shows what's wrong—and what's right—with media coverage of crime. The media have become major players in the criminal justice system and their power increased dramatically in recent years. By studying the media's behavior in specific cases, criticizing their errors and applauding their successes, I hope to raise public awareness of a serious problem in our society, and begin a discussion of possible solutions.

The media are not held accountable for their impact on a criminal case, their effect on the people involved, or even the accuracy of the information they report. This has to change. If the media are going to play an important role in the criminal justice system—and I will argue that they should—they must be more responsible, and more accountable. I'm not talking about new laws, but a new attitude. Decisions by working journalists should be dictated not just by any possible legal restraints (which, under the First Amendment, are minimal to nonexistent), but also by professional ethics, human decency, and common sense—values that are frequently cast aside during high-profile cases.

The media have shown they can cover crime in a way that helps investigations, though. Several cases, like the murder of Martha Moxley, would never have been solved without media attention. The success of *America's Most Wanted* in bringing criminals to justice is partially the result of consulting law enforcement on the cases they depict—and then bringing the actual detectives working the cases to the studio to take calls and follow-up leads. The concerted media silence about the kidnapping of *New York Times* journalist David Rohde quite possibly helped to save his life.

When Rohde returned safely, the impact of his media colleagues' silence as part of efforts to get him back was heralded. The fact that the media were able to perceive the effect their actions could have on efforts to recover Rohde gives me hope that they could extend that understanding to all missing person cases. Why is the life of a missing journalist any different from that of a missing child? They cooperated with law enforcement's efforts to get back one of their own from

Afghanistan. Couldn't they do more of the same for law enforcement in this country?

Meanwhile, other crimes suffer from Media Attention Deficit Disorder. By focusing on real case histories, I will point out the larger lessons that these stories can teach us, and describe how the media can promote justice, but all too often only corrupt it.

I believe that the media can have a largely positive role in the criminal justice system. But things have to change. The media must change their ethos and corrupting practices—it is as simple as that.

The first step in recovery is to admit that you have a problem. In this book, I will expose the truth, in hopes of achieving a new sobriety, a new set of ethics, and a new harness for the media beast that has gotten out of control.

CHAPTER ONE

AMERICAN MURDER MEETS *AMERICAN IDOL*: THE CAYLEE ANTHONY CASE

MURDER IS *VERY* BIG BUSINESS. It has become—let's face it—just another branch of the entertainment industry in this country. As in the rest of the entertainment industry, there are many contenders, but only a few superstars. Just as an entertainer has to have "star quality," a murder has to have the right components of luridness to awaken viewers' ever coarsening sense of horror—and spur fascination bordering on obsession.

According to the FBI's National Crime Information Center (NCIC), 614,925 juveniles under the age of eighteen were registered as missing in the United States in the year 2008. But the one bit of good news is only about 100 of those children who are initially reported as missing actually turn up dead in a given year. Of those, about one every year becomes the object of explosive, saturating media coverage that grips the nation's heart and soul.

In 2008, it was a 2 $1/_2$-year-old girl named Caylee Anthony. She was white, adorable, middle-class, and—according to a myth the media milked for months—not dead but "missing." It was clear very early in the case that Caylee was dead. Some of her hair was found in the wheel-well of the trunk of her mother's abandoned car, which gave off the unmistakable stench of a decomposed body. Despite this, the media ran with the story of a child who was missing and might still be found alive.

This is the story of how the media create alternate realities that serve their quest for ratings, while the criminal investigation that might solve the case is all but derailed. The Caylee Anthony murder case lived up to the cliché minted during the O. J. Simpson trial—it "had it all."

Her young mother, Casey, was beautiful, sexually promiscuous, and seemingly sociopathic. Caylee's grandparents kept an immaculate home, and represented solid middle-class American values—he was an ex-cop and she was a nurse. They couldn't be more "normal," with one exception—George and Cindy's 22-year-old daughter killed their 2 $1/_2$-year-old granddaughter and successfully pretended the little girl was "misplaced" for more than a month before Cindy finally called the cops.

Thus began the notorious, sordid, explosive, and salacious case of the Caylee Anthony murder—a case that epitomized the fusion of murder, mass media, money, fame, and decadence.

———

In case you were in a coma for the second half of 2008 and missed the daily drumbeat of the Caylee Anthony story, here are the highlights.

On Sunday, June 15, Casey Anthony was at her parents' house for Father's Day. Neighbors observed her having a bad fight with her mother, which was nothing new. Casey was a wild party girl who gave straitlaced Cindy no end of grief—she reportedly used drugs and partied hard, and didn't even seem to know who Caylee's father was—while George, quiet and stoic, shuttled between them, trying to keep some peace.

On Monday, June 16, George and Cindy went to their respective jobs: George, a retired cop, worked as a security guard; Cindy, as an RN. George later reported seeing Caylee with Casey when he left for work at 12:30 p.m. He would never see the child alive again.

Casey, meanwhile, went off on what turned into a month-long partying binge, while spinning a tissue of fictions about the whereabouts of her daughter. This included her inventing a fictional babysitter with whom she said she left Caylee.

On June 27, Casey abandoned the family car, which her parents let her use, in a parking lot, claiming it had broken down. Three days later, it was towed to an impound lot. When George picked it up, he noticed a terrible stench in the trunk. Cindy smelled it, too, when he brought it home. She would at first report that it stank like a dead body, then later change her story, attempting to cover up for her daughter, and claim it smelled like old pizza.

On July 15, Caylee Anthony was reported missing. Casey was arrested the next day and charged with child neglect.

At her bond hearing a week later, detectives presented very clear evidence that Caylee Anthony was dead and had been dead for weeks at that point. When they examined the trunk of the car, they found some of the child's hairs in the wheel-well. How many children do you know climb into the trunk of a car to go for a ride with Mommy?

Then there was the cadaver stench. A putrefied human body smells like nothing else in this world—certainly nothing like old pizza. It's a thick stench that instantly engages your gag reflex and causes you physical revulsion on a very deep and instinctual level. Once you've smelled it, you never forget it or mistake it for any other kind of stink.

In a small, closed space, like the trunk of a car in the Florida summer heat, it is indelible. It can't be scrubbed or scoured away. But someone had tried. Fabric freshener sheets, the kind you put in the dryer to scent your laundry, were found in the trunk.

The scent of chloroform was also detected in the trunk. If you've ever watched any old crime movies, you know that chloroform is an anesthetic that can be used to knock a person out.

On top of all that, there were all of Casey's blatant lies about where she'd been, what she'd been doing, and where Caylee had been since June 16. Her bail was set at $500,000, and the police investigated the case as a homicide.

And yet, despite all of that, when the national media descended, they played it up as a missing child case. Over the following weeks and months, they pumped "The Search For Caylee Anthony" into a national obsession.

––––––––––

A closer look at the NCIC missing persons statistics gives you some idea of how many contenders Caylee's story beat out in 2008.

"If they reported every missing child on the news, it's all you would hear on the news," was how an NCIC spokesperson put it. "There wouldn't be time for anything else."

The NCIC collects missing persons data from around the country, based on reports from various state and local agencies. The total number of cases, including both juveniles and adults, in 2008 was roughly 778,000. That same year, almost as many cases—around 745,000—were closed, meaning the missing person was found. Those closed cases include everyone from a child who went missing for one night to people who were reported missing weeks, months, or even years earlier.

At any given time, about 60,000 juveniles are missing in the United States. Roughly half of those have been missing for a year or more. But when we hear "missing children," we tend to think the worst: children abducted by strangers, including pedophiles and other predators. These are the cases the media tend to focus on. But those are actually a very small percentage of missing juveniles. According to national studies conducted for the Department of Justice's Office of Juvenile Justice and Delinquency Prevention (OJJDP), in any given year the vast majority of missing children are either runaways or "throwaways," juveniles kicked out of their homes by parents or other caretakers. Fewer than one in ten missing juveniles at any given time was abducted, and most of those were abducted by a family member— for instance, one parent snatching a child from another parent after losing custody in a divorce. Of those 60,000 juveniles who are missing as you read this, probably fewer than 3 percent, maybe 1,000 of them, are believed to have been abducted by strangers, according to the OJJDP.

The NCIC database crunches the numbers its own way but gets the same results. Of the 614,925 missing juveniles registered by the NCIC in 2008, about 13,000, or roughly 2 percent, were categorized as "endangered," which is defined as "missing under circumstances indicating that they may be in physical danger."

Again—the very good news is that of all those thousands of juveniles who go missing in a year, only a tiny minority are found dead:

about 100 a year nationwide, according to the National Center for Missing & Exploited Children.

So why do we hear so much about that tiny minority of cases—so much so that every time we hear the words "missing child," we think the worst?

Obviously, like the FBI spokesperson said, the media couldn't make news out of all 600,000-plus missing juvenile cases in 2008. They're going to focus on the most spectacular, suspenseful, grisly, sexy, twisted, tragic ones—that small percentage of cases where it's possible the child was murdered—like Caylee Anthony. NCIC data suggest that in the month of July 2008, when Caylee Anthony was reported missing by her grandmother, there were probably about 3,000 other juveniles reported missing in the state of Florida. But only Caylee's story had the right ingredients to be blown up into national news.

What are those ingredients? Think of it as "American Murder Meets *American Idol*." Ideally, both the murder victim and the suspect are attractive and telegenic. The relatives too, if possible. The other elements that go into the mix are a mysterious combination of seeming *just like us*—average Americans—and yet totally unlike us. They can't be unattractive, overweight, uneducated, or poor. And above all else, they must be white.

After the O. J. Simpson case, asking the American mass media to go back to a more sober, fact-oriented, and investigative kind of crime coverage would be like asking a band of silver prospectors to abandon the Comstock Lode in Nevada's Virginia mountains in 1859. With O. J., silver *and* gold were struck, in unimaginable quantities. The media will never turn back until everything has been mined, until the audience turns away, or until things become so catastrophic in the country that people actually have to turn their attention to their own survival.

I was central to the O. J. Simpson spectacle and lived it from the inside. I have been on both sides of the strange freak show where murder meets media and all hell breaks loose. I have seen how the entertainment juggernaut moves in and overtakes a murder investigation—creating chaos, confusion, hype, and hysteria. The criminal investigation becomes corrupted or even paralyzed, but the rewards in the coffers of the mass media and entertainment complex are so vast that no power on earth can rein them in once they have a case that has "legs."

Just like every other arm of the entertainment industry, the Murder Business imposes absolute production values, seeds obsession into the national psyche, locks in the audience, and expands the product line as far and long as possible.

They have countless ways of doing this. When, for example, Caylee's skeletal remains were finally found by Roy Kronk in December 2008, his background and life became fresh fodder for the story. He was paid a sum of $20,000 by one of the major networks to come on TV and be interviewed about his grisly find. Of course, they were paying for the *licensing* of the blurry photo he took of the swampy area where Caylee's remains were found, not the interview. Yeah, right.

This peak moment capped a frenzy that had been going full tilt for six months, while the grandparents stonewalled, while the suspect lied, while her legal dream team crumbled, and while increasingly outlandish scenarios were peddled to the hooked audience about the fate of the child.

Caylee's disappearance hit the national news in July 2008. By August, the media-besieged family had a public relations spokesman representing them. He would quit, or be fired, in November, following allegations that he'd pocketed money NBC thought it was paying for Anthony family photos. But everybody connected to the case seemed to be striking deals, and lots of others hopped on the gravy train, too. Home videos of the child started to hit the media market, selling for astronomical sums. There was a T-shirt with Casey's mugshot on it and a quote from her first angry jailhouse call ("Waste, Huge Waste"); another shirt mocked the imaginary nanny "Zanny"; there was a Casey Anthony voodoo doll on eBay, and even a doll "inspired by" Caylee Anthony, called the "Caylee Sunshine Doll," that sings "You Are My Sunshine" when you press its belly-button. This sold for $29.99 online. It was briefly taken off the market due to complaints, but was soon brought back "by popular demand."

Beyond the crush of relentless media coverage on network and cable television, a new media epiphenomenon developed: Youtube clips of Caylee Anthony gurgling, dancing, and playing with her mother in various stages of toddlerhood. And then there were the photos and video clips of her mother in various stages of gyrating decadence, apparently enjoying South Florida's disco-and-Jello-shots nightlife while her only daughter was missing and possibly dead. She became known as the "hot-tot mom."

The Very Cute Innocent Child and the Very Bad Wicked Mother had now been minted as characters in this drama, and products— clips or pictures—that fed those images were in high demand. Hundreds of thousands watched each Caylee Anthony clip, and commented passionately about each gurgle and word she uttered. Thousands wrote in and swore they loved her as much as if she were their own child, and Caylee Kitsch was born—countless video montages with images of the little girl superimposed with roses, birds, animals, and sad music.

Everybody settled into a comfortable seat to watch the show, which not only must go on, but on and on and on, spinning off the very axis of facts and forensic evidence that, in the normal world, would bring the case to a screeching halt. This is the first real problem of Murder in the age of Mass Media—doubts, mysteries, and questions fuel the fire like oxygen.

The second problem is that law enforcement and media work at cross purposes. They want opposite things. Law enforcement want to solve and close a case as quickly and effectively as possible. The media want to *prolong* the whole thing as long as possible, and everything they do contributes overtly or covertly to that goal. This is why they don't investigate, ask tough questions of suspects, try to eliminate speculative scenarios, or do anything at all to contribute to solving anything. Every Tom, Dick, and Harry who wants to chime in with an absurd new angle or wrinkle is given tail-wind by the blowing machines. Every family member who has any unexpressed or not yet exhausted set of emotions is invited on TV shows again and again, while the pot gets stirred and stirred. They manufacture *questions,* but never try to *answer* them, even when the answers are right at their feet. They pretend victims are alive even when it is patently clear there is no chance—just to keep the story alive, to maintain the taut bubble of tension that is required, as in every soap opera, to keep the viewers hooked.

I'm sure every news producer in national TV knows that almost all of the 100 or so missing kids who are found dead every year were murdered within *a few hours* of their disappearance. Not six months, or six weeks, or six days. A few hours.

This Murder Business makes a mockery out of plain facts, evidence, and logic. It ropes entire families into the circus, making it impossible for them to live their lives at all, never mind process their grief. I was not surprised when I heard that George Anthony, a retired cop, had become suicidal and had to be hospitalized at the peak of the media frenzy in January 2009. Caylee's remains had been identified, and Casey charged with her murder, a month earlier. George had allegedly been sending suicidal text messages to family members, and had himself been reported missing after failing to show up for a meeting with his and Cindy's lawyer. He turned up in a Daytona motel. He was later released from care in time to attend Caylee's memorial service in February 2009.

Nobody is honest with the families. The media exploits them ruthlessly to gain their sound-bites—seducing and then abandoning them. They are seduced by the very expert legions of competing TV producers who fly them to New York and put them up in five-star hotels, with lavish meals, Broadway tickets, and in some cases, large checks for the "fair use" of some object, photo, or video they have in their possession.

They convince them that they *care.* That may be the most insidious part of it all—that unctuous deception. Detectives have a clipped, burnished, straight-shooting, professional demeanor for a *reason.* Well, for many reasons. One is that we consider it unprofessional to wallow in the emotions of a tragedy that you are there to solve, period. You say, "I'm sorry for your loss," and that is it. Then you get to work. And whom do you work for? You work for the victim. You're not working for ratings, advertisers, audiences, or any of that—you are the sole and singular advocate for the one who has no voice—the victim—and that is where you place your entire loyalty.

In the case of Caylee Anthony, I found myself in the position of having to tell the grandparents, George and Cindy, what they already knew—the truth. All the evidence in the case suggested that Caylee Anthony was killed in their home on June 16, 2008.

I was dispatched by FOX down to Orlando, Florida, to the quiet suburban street where the Anthonys live, to report on the developments of the case in August 2008, as it reached a media frenzy of O. J. proportions.

Outside, the media hordes were packed along the suburban streets with their reporters endlessly pretending the search for Caylee Anthony could "bring her home" any day or at any moment, with the help of flyers, posters, search teams, and volunteers. I couldn't believe what was going on. Every detective taking even a cursory look at the evidence knew the child was dead, and it didn't take a rocket scientist to figure it out, either.

The first evening on the trip, as I prepared a report for Greta Van Susteren's show from outside George and Cindy Anthony's house, I was told by Steph Watts, Greta's producer, that Cindy Anthony had called and asked us to meet her and George at their house after the broadcast. At 11:00 p.m. I went over, and we sat down to talk in their living room. We stayed about two hours. I was struck by a strange disparity. Their daughter was in jail, their granddaughter was missing, and yet their house looked like it was ready for a *House & Garden* photo shoot. It was beyond immaculate. It was absolutely spotless, as if nobody lived there. It was surreal. Everything was perfectly ordered, everything in its proper place. *Yet,* I thought to myself, *how could these people—who might be considered organized to the point of having OCD—not realize their granddaughter was missing for a whole month?* Something was odd.

Both of them wore perfectly clean, pressed clothes. George sat back on the sofa with his shoulders rolled forward a little bit, in a posture of quiet despair. He barely said anything. Cindy, by contrast, leaned forward and spoke animatedly. Throughout the conversation, I listened closely and looked around. The whole time Cindy was talking around and through the fantasy that Caylee would be found. Here you had two people—a cop and a nurse—who both know exactly what a decomposing body smells like. There is no mistaking that smell. They smelled it in the trunk of their car, yet they clung to the story that their grandchild was "missing." Their delusion—primarily Cindy's—was understandable, but unnecessary in light of the evidence. Yet the media continued to enable it.

Why had they asked to meet me? They said it was because they wondered if I could help them. At a certain point, during a lull in the conversation, I had to approach them as a detective, not a member of the news media. I looked straight at them and said gently,

"You know Caylee is dead."

There was a silence.

George looked at me and he just bobbed his head up and down, as if to say yes. Cindy cried quietly. I got the feeling George knew that the baby was dead and that Cindy also knew but was blocking it out. The police absolutely knew they had a dead child here. And if it weren't for the media manipulating George and Cindy's delusions, refusing to challenge them in things as glaringly obvious as the smell of decomposed body in their car, the "Caylee-is-missing" myth never would have come to life. A lot of time was wasted on it, because the media gave it such legitimacy. The media myth wasted the time and resources of the detectives.

Looking for a missing child is very different than looking for a body and a crime scene. With each passing day, witnesses' memories are corrupted, and vital clues obscured. Meanwhile, constant coverage results in thousands of false tips that the detectives are then required to investigate, no matter how crazy. And cases like these really bring out the wackos.

Cindy, a nurse, was clinging to the delusion that the stench in her car was not that of a corpse but perhaps a rotten pizza. And Caylee's hairs found in the trunk? I don't mean to sound callous, but how many people find locks of their granddaughter's hair in the trunk of their car? Elephants in the room, you might say. But the media reported the flimsy, ludicrous myth, for months and months, that Caylee might be alive, because they wanted what they always want. They wanted the story to "grow legs." It doesn't do that if certain undeniable facts emerge too soon. It spoils the tension and the build-up necessary for a story to grow *real* legs.

———

I went back to the Anthonys' the next day. We walked outside in their backyard and around their pool. Lee, Casey's 36-year-old brother, was with us. Like his mother, he clung to the delusion that Casey was innocent. In one of the most repulsive twists in the case, rumors spread that Lee was Caylee's father; the FBI even gave him a paternity test, which proved that he was not.

I focused their attention on June 16, the last day the family saw Caylee alive. Cindy had left for work that morning, George at

12:30 p.m., leaving Casey and Caylee alone in the house. A neighbor had reported that Casey borrowed a shovel from him that day. Cindy said she'd probably wanted to dig up some of the bamboo that was overgrown all over the yard. I found this unbelievable. From everything we knew about Casey, she wasn't the backyard gardening type. It sounded to me like the only time she lifted a finger was to have her nails done.

The neighbor also said he saw Casey back the family car into the garage, which he found odd. She usually just drove it straight in.

I noticed that the ladder was in the pool. "Is that always there?" I asked.

"No," Cindy replied. "I swam with Caylee on Sunday, and when we were done I pulled it up."

That made sense to me. She wouldn't have left the ladder down for her two-year-old granddaughter to wander out and climb down into the water.

"But when I came home Monday, it was there," Cindy added.

So someone obviously used the pool on Monday.

Lee was so intent on proving Casey's innocence that he was playing amateur detective. He'd obtained her cell phone records, looking for clues. He showed them to me. They showed an unusual flurry of activity on that Monday afternoon. Casey had called her mother and father several times. None of the calls had been answered.

To me—and I'm sure to any other experienced detective who heard and saw all this—it added up to an unavoidable conclusion. Caylee Anthony died sometime during the day on June 16, at her grandparents' house. Exactly how that happened, we'll probably never know. Casey immediately started to think of how to dispose of her daughter's body. She tried calling both her parents—to find out, I believe, when they were planning to be home. She knew her mother worked a normal day shift, while George wouldn't be back until after midnight. She was just checking to make sure they weren't going to deviate this day, and come home early and surprise her—especially her mother.

She borrowed the neighbor's shovel, possibly thinking she'd bury the child in her parents' backyard. Then, realizing how stupid that was, she backed the car into the garage and opened the trunk. She stuffed Caylee's body in a large plastic bag from the garage. (Later, when Caylee's skeletal remains were found, they were with the same make of bag the Anthonys had in their garage.) She put the child in the trunk and drove off.

However we envision the next month, it's a horror story. Maybe Casey "staged" her daughter's body somewhere—that is, stashed it in a temporary hiding place, while thinking about a more permanent one. Maybe she even just left the child rotting in the trunk as she drove around from one party to the next. Either way, by the time she abandoned the car on July 27, Caylee's body had so putrefied that it leaked fluids in the trunk, leaving the hideous stench that no fabric fresheners could ever get rid of.

It's extremely hard to imagine a young mother handling the putrefied remains of her child. It's a messy and revolting business. About three hours after death, the process of rigor mortis starts, stiffening the muscles, and lasts up to seventy-two hours. After that, putrefaction begins. Bacteria break down cell walls. Gravity causes the fluids in the body to collect at the lowest point. Gases build up and rupture the corpse. Shut up in a plastic bag, in the trunk of a car or stashed somewhere else, in the Florida summer heat, little Caylee's remains would have been reduced to a putrid jelly and bones within a month. Sometime on or before July 27, Casey hauled the plastic bag out of the trunk, leaving it in a nearby wooded lot, where it was later found. But in the process, some of Caylee's hair and fluids were left behind in the car. Unable to get rid of the stink, Casey simply and stupidly abandoned the car—for her father to reclaim, and instantly recognize the hideous stench of death.

And it all started on June 16, as I was able to deduce from my two visits with the Anthonys. Being able to narrow the timeline like that is very important in a homicide investigation. It allows detectives to focus on specific activities, ask witnesses specific questions about precise times and places, review specific records, and not let the investigation get bogged down in useless pursuits.

The media, of course, prefer to *widen* the focus of their "investigations" as broadly as possible. They want a big, loose timeline filled with "leads" and "possible suspects" and "persons of interest"—a story with legs. They didn't want a grim and depressing Search for Caylee Anthony's Body, but a suspenseful, heart-rending Search for Caylee Anthony. A story they could drag out for months, long after it was clear to me, the police, and every realistic observer or participant, that the child was dead.

For the news media, the crime fans, the morbid merchandisers, and the cultists who fetishize missing children—especially angelic-looking girls—the Caylee Anthony story was the biggest thing since JonBenét. Nancy Grace, television host for CNN, got a solid six months of nightly programs out of it. But when Caylee was found and Casey indicted in December 2008, everyone knew the gravy train was pulling in to its final destination. It was time for a new story.

For a while, the disappearance of Haleigh Cummings looked like it might be that story. Some of the linkages were almost too good to be true. Her name rhymed with Caylee's. She was also an adorable little blonde. She also lived in Florida. And the very morning Haleigh was reported missing from her trailer home in Satsuma—February 10, 2009—Caylee's memorial service was taking place about 100 miles south in Orlando. What more could the media ask for?

In other ways, though, Caylee and Haleigh were worlds apart. Where the Anthonys were a "normal" middle class family torn apart by murder and grief, Haleigh's story turned out to be a descent to the lowest rungs of white America, the very definition of trailer-park trash. The story of Haleigh's disappearance quickly turned as murky and swampy as the central Florida area where she lived—and undoubtedly died. It was more suited for the *Jerry Springer Show* than network news. This was the underbelly of the American underbelly.

Ronald Cummings, aged twenty-five, worked the late shift operating a crane at a bridge fabricating firm. His two children—daughter Haleigh, five, and son Ron Jr., four—lived with him in his double-wide trailer home in the small Putnam County community of Satsuma. Their mother, Crystal Sheffield, whom Ronald had never married, did not live with them. But his current girlfriend, the 17-year-old Misty Croslin, did.

Around 3:00 a.m. on the morning of February 10, Misty purportedly got out of bed to use the bathroom. She discovered that Haleigh was not in her own bed—a small mattress on the floor of the trailer home's "master" bedroom. Searching the house, she found the back door standing open. She was calling Ron on his cell phone when he pulled into the driveway. He told her to call 911 while he searched the house again.

At the start, police and the media pursued a straightforward abduction theory. Convicted sex offenders in the area were canvassed. A pedophile cousin of Misty's was eyed.

But questions soon arose about Misty's testimony first, then about her character—and Ronald's. By March, Crystal Sheffield had hired a lawyer and, among other things, was telling Nancy Grace that Ronald had physically abused both her and the children. The cast of dark, unsavory characters widened to include William "Cobra" Staubs, a private investigator and bounty hunter hired by Crystal's lawyer; Jerome Williams, a drug dealer and felon; Amber Brooks, an associate of Williams' and another of Ronald's former girlfriends, who had a son with him; and Kristina Rene "Nay-Nay" Prevatt, another of Williams' friends, who had once allegedly tried to snatch her own daughter, Destiny, from her "baby daddy." Misty and Amber were allegedly rivals for Ron's affections, and had almost come to blows at least once. Misty and Nay Nay had allegedly gone on a three-day drugs and sex binge with another man, Greg "White Boy" Page, the weekend before Haleigh's Monday night disappearance.

The more America heard about these people, the less we wanted to know. Meanwhile, little Haleigh was still missing. Then, a month after her disappearance, Ronald and Misty got married. The ceremony was held in a friend's backyard, because their church disapproved of the union. So did some observers of the case, pointing out that as man and wife, Misty and Ron could not be called to testify against each other. Ron and Misty flew straight to New York to appear on the *Today Show* the morning after the wedding. Interviewed by Meredith Vieira, Ron looked petulant and Misty was shifty.

And little Haleigh was still missing. But unlike the Caylee case, Haleigh failed to ignite the constant and passionate interest of the

American mass media or its audience. It had turned into too much of a white-trash nightmare, *too much* of a freak show. Viewers can take the bizarre, frightening underbelly of White America only in small doses in a careful context, as guests in Jerry Springer or Maury Povich's circus acts, or when they're anonymous figures being arrested, with their faces digitally obscured, on *Cops*. Gazing directly into Misty Croslin-Cummings' disturbingly vacant eyes, and being stared down by the tight-jawed and petulant Ronald Cummings, was too much raw, unpleasant truth for the average viewer to stomach. There were no sympathetic characters in the story, except for Haleigh herself, and yet no clear and easily despised villains like Casey Anthony, either. There was just darkness and murk and swampy confusion.

A colleague from one of the networks called me from Satsuma and urged me not to make the trip if FOX asked me to go. "Everybody here is high on something," he said, "and everyone is a nightmare to interview and put on TV."

Soon the story faded. The media pulled up stakes and retreated.

And Haleigh was still missing.

———————

Another child disappeared in Florida around the same time Haleigh did. On January 11, Adji Desir vanished while playing outside his grandmother's residence in a place called Farm Workers Village, which offers subsidized rental housing for Florida farm laborers, in Immokalee, east of Naples.

He had even more than social class going against him. For one thing, he was a boy. For another, he was black.

He was also a sweet and innocent-looking six-year-old. In addition, he was a "special needs" child, barely able to speak, and said to have the intellect of a two-year-old. His parents were very, very poor—immigrants who couldn't even speak English, hardly ready for their *Today Show* interview. Police searched for Adji. Nancy Grace and *America's Most Wanted* mentioned the case. Psychics threw their two cents in. But little Adji made barely a dent on the national media or consciousness. His mother and stepdad did some local TV interviews, speaking in French. They looked like decent, hard-working, long-suffering people. The police ended their physical search of the surrounding area and fell back on waiting for leads, which didn't come. Adji soon disappeared from the media as quietly and irrevocably as he apparently had from this earth.

In more ways than one, it was Adji Desir's misfortune not to have been born a pretty, blonde white girl. Black children account for about 35 percent of missing juveniles; black males, about 16 percent. But they don't get much attention from the media, or generate anything like the maudlin, cultish love-fests that pour out for a Caylee or a JonBenét. Even Haleigh didn't measure up. Right race, right color of hair, right sex, but wrong class.

The Search For Caylee Anthony played out in the national media for six months. The search for Haleigh Cummings faded out of the national spotlight in a few weeks. Adji was barely a blip on the national media screen, gone in days.

During the O. J. Simpson trial, national media gleefully took the defense team's bait in painting me as a racist because their client was black, as was a majority of the jury. But their own racism is deep, insidious, and systemic. They demonstrate it every time they blow life into a murder story, and make abundantly clear to their viewers that not all lives are equally precious. It is the American media itself that holds in place ancient hierarchies dictating that social class trumps everything else. Ask yourself this: Has the media ever—ever—taken a black child and converted him or her into a beloved lost child—a Jon-Benét or a Caylee? How about a young black woman? Can you name even one?

I rest my case.

CHAPTER TWO

KILLER COP: DREW PETERSON

IN MAY 2009, DREW PETERSON, a former police sergeant in the Chicago suburb of Bolingbrook, IL, was arrested and charged with the 2004 murder of his third wife, Kathleen. He thought he had committed the perfect crime—and he almost had. We know he thought it was the perfect crime because he allegedly said so at the time to his fourth wife, Stacy. Stacy disappeared in 2007 and is still missing as I write this.

Just as in Caylee Anthony's case, media and local law enforcement worked at cross-purposes. Unlike the Anthony case, however, this was one time when that wasn't entirely a bad thing. Drew Peterson almost got away with murder (and may still, as the outcome of his case is still pending as I write this), because he knew the weaknesses of the local law enforcement system that would investigate and prosecute him. By putting pressure and a spotlight on that system, the media, or at least some in the media, actually helped put Peterson behind bars.

Soon after Stacy Peterson disappeared on October 29, 2007, FOX sent me to Bolingbrook, Illinois, where I looked into the case with FOX news producers Steph Watts and Cory Howard. I wasn't there in any official law enforcement capacity. I didn't have a badge. I couldn't get search warrants or ask for a wiretap or direct a team of detectives to canvass a neighborhood for clues.

All I had to work with was my experience, common sense, and a motivation to see justice served. But then again, those skills are what a detective relies on most. You can't create clues out of thin air. You sift through whatever evidence presents itself, follow up potential leads, use your brains and your sixth sense, and build your investigation from every available detail.

―――――――――――

When you look at his biography, Drew Peterson starts out sounding like the All-American guy. Born in 1954, he went into the Army right from high school, and from there to the Bolingbrook Police Department, where he once won an officer of the year award for his work on the narcotics squad. He would be on the force for almost thirty years.

There was an obvious pattern to Drew Peterson's marriages. Too bad his last two wives didn't recognize it.

His first wife, Carol Brown, met him at their high school prom. They divorced after six years, with Carol citing his infidelity as the cause. His second wife, Victoria, left him after ten years when she found out he was seeing Kathleen Savio. Drew and Kathleen were married two months after his divorce from Victoria.

Drew and Kathleen were together from May 1992 to October 2003. Toward the end of their marriage, Drew began seeing Stacy Cales. In the midst of a lot of bitter fighting over the division of assets and the custody of their two sons, Drew and Kathleen's divorce was finalized on October 10, 2003. He married Stacy on October 18. He was forty-nine, she was nineteen.

On March 1, 2004, while returning his sons to their mother after a visitation, Drew Peterson found Kathleen's door locked and got no response. He called on a neighbor for help, and the neighbor called a locksmith. When the neighbor entered the home—Drew let the neighbor go in first, saying later that he "didn't want any trouble"—she found Kathleen's lifeless body in a dry bathtub, her hair soaked with blood.

Because Peterson was a Bolingbrook cop, the investigation of Kathleen's death was handled by the Illinois State Police (ISP). That way, supposedly, there wouldn't be any conflict of interest. After a brief investigation by the ISP and an autopsy, the county coroner's office ruled Kathleen's death an accidental drowning.

Three and a half years later, on October 29, 2007, Stacy Peterson, twenty-three years old, was reported missing. Although Peterson claimed that Stacy had left him to be with another man, her family insisted that she would never have abandoned her two young children.

Stacy's disappearance rekindled interest in Kathleen's death. You didn't need to be Sherlock Holmes to begin wondering if Drew Peterson was not only a serial husband and philanderer, but a budding serial wife-killer.

The national media converged on Bolingbrook. It was a story that had potential. The Petersons were white and middle class. The missing ex-wife was young and pretty. The husband seemed more than happy to talk to the media, and he was good at it—affable, engaging, and intelligent. In the first few weeks after Stacy's disappearance, he spoke to Greta Van Susteren, Geraldo Rivera, and Matt Lauer. He made the cover of *People* magazine. You could see he enjoyed the attention.

Meanwhile, I arrived to look into the case for FOX. Working with my news producers Steph and Cory, I familiarized myself with the local layout and the players in Bolingbrook. I tried to get my hands on potentially useful documents. I met with family members and I looked for leads. We got no help from the Illinois State Police. They wouldn't even return my calls. However, I quickly developed a good relationship with the Bolingbrook police and their chief, Ray McGuiry. But McGuiry hadn't been in Bolingbrook when Kathleen died (he came on as chief in 2005), and now he wasn't much more in the loop with the ISP than I was.

We got a break early in November when the Savio family gave Greta's show a copy of the autopsy report the medical examiner had filed on Kathleen back in March 2004. It was only four pages, documenting a very cursory examination. It immediately raised all kinds of questions for me. I couldn't see how anyone could read the document and blithely conclude that Kathleen Savio had died accidentally. To me, it looked like a homicide right away.

I wasn't alone. In New York, forensic pathologist Michael Baden read the same report and said point-blank on Greta Van Susteren's show, "This is a homicide."

Under "External Evidence of Injury," for starters, the report listed a blunt laceration on the left scalp, where she may have hit her head falling down in the tub. Only it seemed to be on the wrong side of her head. The other possibility was that somebody hit her with a blunt object.

There were oval contusions on the abdomen, where somebody might have been striking her with something like a flashlight—maybe the same blunt instrument that lacerated her scalp. There were abrasions on her right wrist, where somebody might have been pulling or dragging her. There were parallel contusions on the mid-shins, an abrasion on the left elbow, and a circular abrasion on the first finger of the right hand.

Now to me, this did not add up to someone falling down in the tub, hitting her head, and then drowning. It sounded more like a fight—someone who was beaten on the head in another room, then dragged by her right wrist into the bathroom, her limbs bumping into doorjambs and such along the way. If I were the detective on the case, I'd at least want to look into the possibility.

(And at that point, I hadn't yet read the testimony of the EMT workers who arrived on the scene, who reported that there were no towels in the bathroom. She was going to take a bath or shower with no towels? There were no clothes in the bathroom. Where had she undressed? The shampoo bottles on the side of the tub weren't disturbed, the way you'd expect if she'd slipped and reached out to catch herself.)

This was the report that was presented to the Will County coroner's jury who ruled her death an accidental drowning. I really wanted to know who this jury was, what their expertise was, and how this whole coroner's jury system worked.

Cory and I got in touch with the Will County coroner's office and made an appointment. When we arrived, we didn't expect the coroner, Patrick O'Neil, to speak to us. Why should he? We were from the media, nobody he was compelled to speak to, and a lot of questions were starting to be raised about how he'd handled the Savio case.

Michael Baden had flatly contradicted the coroner jury's determination on national television. When a local official in a sleepy town suddenly finds his actions being questioned in the national spotlight, he tends to think more about covering his ass than showing his face. We figured at best we'd speak to an assistant, who might at least explain to us, curtly, how the coroner's jury system worked.

So we were very surprised when O'Neil himself ushered us into his office. He was friendly, almost ingratiating, eager to talk, eager to be of help. I figured he knew his ass was in a sling, and he was trying to get out in front of the story.

In Will County, he explained, the coroner is an elected official. If someone wants to run for coroner in Will County and he gets enough votes, he's the coroner. No special knowledge or expertise is required. O'Neil made a point of telling us he was a third-generation coroner. His father and grandfather had held the job before him. Sounded to me like he'd got the job more out of name recognition than any special skills.

"Do you have any medical training? Are you qualified as a medical examiner?" I asked.

"Well no," he said, "but that's not our system. If we need an autopsy, we hire a medical examiner to do it."

"But you have to know you need an autopsy before you can hire that person," I said. "Who makes that determination if there's no full-time medical examiner?" Normally, the responding detective decides how to handle such a case.

"Well, you have a death that could be a homicide or an accident," he replied. "So you impanel a coroner's jury, six people who are picked just like jurors in court trials. They are presented the case and then they take a vote."

"These are just six average Joes from off the street?" I asked.

"That's right. Six citizens, impaneled just like any other kind of jury."

"And how much of a presentation of the evidence do they get?"

"The whole thing takes about an hour," he said. "It could take a couple hours at the most."

Actually, one of the jurors on the Savio case later said that in fact, they spent only thirty to forty-five minutes on her. They had a number of cases to get through that day and didn't linger much on any one of them. But I didn't know that yet when I spoke to O'Neil.

"So let me get this straight," I said. "Somebody dies. You don't know if it's a homicide or an accident. You pull six average citizens off a bench at a bus stop, people with probably no medical or forensic experience. You present the evidence, and in the period of 'a couple of hours at the most,' you expect them to render an intelligent verdict on whether this death was a homicide, suicide, or accident? People who may never even have seen a dead body are ruling on the cause of death?"

"Yeah, that's the system," he said.

"Are you *kidding* me?" I asked. "No offense, Mr. O'Neil, but an idiot could read this autopsy report and see this is a homicide. You don't need a coroner's jury. Why didn't the detective rule that this was a homicide?"

"It just didn't add up," he said. "They weren't sure. It looked like an accident."

I read the "External Evidence of Injury" list aloud to O'Neil.

"Mr. O'Neil, do you think this is an accidental death?"

"That's what the coroner's jury determined," he said.

"I didn't ask that. Do *you* think this sounds like an accidental death?"

"Well, I wasn't sure."

And it kept getting better. Or rather, worse. The ISP officer who presented the evidence to this coroner's jury, Herbert Hardy, admitted at the inquest that he was not the lead detective on the case. He was not the lead detective's partner. He was just some other detective the ISP sent to present the case to the inquest. He admitted that although he was at the scene, he never saw Kathleen's body, and did not go to the autopsy, either. He couldn't render an opinion about any of her injuries because he didn't see them. He didn't talk to Drew Peterson.

And it gets even better—or worse—still. In interviewing one of the jurors, Walter Lee James, Cory learned that another juror that day was a cop. Not long after our talk with O'Neil, Cory got Mr. James on Greta's show. Greta asked him about this.

"There was a police officer on the panel," James said, "and he indicated at the time he knew or knew of Peterson. And he indicated to the panel that he thought that Peterson was a good policeman. He was charitable and helped his neighbors, and so on and so forth. So I think that—I think that might have influenced some of the panel members, but I don't know that for sure."

This was astounding. Had O'Neil never heard of *voir dire*—the need to avoid potential bias when determining if a crime has occurred? When he selected his jury, he never asked them what their occupations were? If he did, and one of them said he was a cop, it didn't occur to O'Neil to excuse this man from serving on a jury that was to determine if a fellow cop's ex-wife's questionable death was an accident or homicide? He didn't see a possible conflict of interest there?

Clearly this "coroner's jury" was an archaic, absurd system. It dates back to Medieval England and should have been left there. But there may be a reason some local jurisdictions have stuck with it. They ask these civilians with no special competence to make these decisions for them, *so they can blame them if it goes south*. Which O'Neil seemed to be doing in this case.

As he asked me in his office, "the coroner's jury said it was an accident. What do you think I should have done?"

"Are you bound by their decisions?" I asked him.

"No."

"Then you should have said, 'I'm the coroner. I've got the authority. I'm not so sure this was an accident. I want it investigated as a possible homicide.'"

The Savio family thought it was suspicious from the beginning. But they didn't have the right kind of knowledge of forensics to say whether or not it was a homicide. They needed expert help. Three years later, only as a result of Stacy Peterson's disappearance and subsequent media queries, they were getting it.

National media were bearing down on this preposterous system. On November 8, Will County state's attorney James Glasgow announced that there was reason to believe that Kathleen Savio's death was not accidental, and ordered that her body be exhumed and re-examined. Drew Peterson was openly named as a suspect. He resigned from the Bolingbrook police department.

O'Neil, who I suspected was now very eager to get on the right side of this story, hired a competent forensic pathologist, Dr. Larry Blum, to do the new autopsy. The Savio family hired Michael Baden to conduct his own independent examination.

On November 13, after decomposing in the grave for three years, Kathleen's body was exhumed. And despite the heavy decomposition, both Blum and Baden determined that her death was a homicide.

It was clear to me that Kathleen Savio's death was not really investigated in 2004. The Illinois State Police went through the motions—went to the scene, talked to some people, did an autopsy—but they didn't do anything like a proper investigation.

I knew this because three years later I was asking questions they must not have asked at the time, and getting answers they couldn't have considered when they so quickly decided that Kathleen's death was accidental.

For instance, Drew Peterson said that when he brought their sons to Kathleen's home, he found the door locked. That's why he asked a neighbor to call a locksmith.

Now, maybe he didn't have a key. Maybe Kathleen had changed the locks.

But first, ask yourself this: if you're so concerned that your ex-wife, the mother of your two children, may have come to some harm behind that locked door, would you really stand around outside and wait for a locksmith? Or would you kick in the door? Drew Peterson was a cop. He knew how to use a size 12 search warrant.

And why did he ask the neighbor to call the locksmith? Didn't he have a cell phone?

Pondering these questions, I interviewed Victoria, his second wife. She told me an interesting thing: during their marriage, Drew Peterson went to locksmith's school. She said he always carried a professional locksmith's set with him after that.

So he could have picked that lock. Instead, he called a neighbor for help.

Why? *Because you can't be the person who finds the body if you're the murderer.*

What you can do—what you have to do—is have someone else discover the body. So here's this cop, who had a gun on him or in his car, and is supposedly worried that something's wrong inside the house. There may be a burglar in there, or a rapist, or someone holding Kathleen hostage, or who knows. Does he pull his gun and go in there first? No. He sends the neighbor in first, while he waits outside.

Then, when the cops arrive, Drew Peterson asks them to take him inside so he can identify the body. No cop should have agreed to that, because if you're a suspect and the cops allow you to walk into the crime scene, you contaminate it. You've created an excuse for any of your hair, fibers from your clothes, footprints, or fingerprints found there. Maybe you left that evidence when you were perpetrating the crime; maybe you left it when you were identifying the body. Forensically, it's now useless to the prosecution.

Drew Peterson knew that. Too bad the other cops didn't.

Too bad for Stacy Peterson, I mean. Because if the cops and everyone else had been doing their jobs in 2004, Drew Peterson wouldn't have been free to kill Stacy in 2007.

Was it because they lacked the tools, the training, or the brains? Was it just laziness? Did they just not care? Or were they compromised?

Was it corruption, or just incompetent business-as-usual? In some ways, business-as-usual is more disturbing than corruption. Maybe these investigators weren't corrupt in the traditional sense; they were just protecting the good-old-boy network. They relaxed the rules at the crime scene because the shocked and bereaved ex-husband was a fellow cop. In half-heartedly investigating the case, they looked the other way, because they didn't want to see that the murderer was one of their own. Not hard to believe in a suburb of Chicago, in a state then governed by Ron Blagojevich.

One thing is indisputable: when you don't do your duty and investigate a homicide, for whatever reason, that means a murderer is still at large, and may kill again. The police did not investigate Kathleen Savio's death, and I think we can say with fair certainty that three years later another woman, Stacy Peterson, paid for that negligence with her life.

_____

By looking into and questioning the preposterous coroner's jury system, and bringing the TV spotlight to bear on it, we helped move a piece or two of the puzzle into place.

At the same time, Steph Watts and I found another lead to follow. One miserably cold morning in mid-November, with a damp and heavy snow falling, he and I sat in a rental car outside our hotel. We sipped bad coffee in paper cups and leafed through the morning papers we'd picked up in the lobby.

We saw an article in that morning's *Chicago Sun-Times*, reporting that a few months before she disappeared, Stacy Peterson had confided to an unnamed minister at her church that she feared for her life.

"Well *that's* interesting," Steph and I both said. We chugged our coffees, fired up the car, and headed off to Stacy's church.

We met two ministers at the church. One was white, maybe fifty years old, and the other was black, younger, maybe thirty-five. They were courteous but guarded with us. I suspected that the ISP had told them not to be talking to media. We asked our questions anyway. Was the unnamed minister cited in this article there? No, he'd left the church to start up a new congregation. Could they tell us where that was? No.

Fine. I went back to the car and Googled "new minister" and "Bolingbrook" on my Blackberry. The name Neil Schori popped up, mentioning that he'd left the church where we just were, and giving the address of his new church.

The first line of investigations is often that simple. In the old days, you called 411 or flipped open the White Pages. Today, you Google.

We drove to his church, and I asked a janitor if Pastor Schori was available. Soon, a very tall, muscular young man in chinos and a knit turtleneck sweater greeted me. He didn't look like your stereotypical minister. He looked more like a Nordic fisherman.

He smiled. "How'd you guys find me?"

"Well, you're on the Internet," I said.

I was surprised we were the first. Bolingbrook was crawling with national and local media people. Presumably at least some of them had seen that article in the morning paper. I knew for a fact that every single one of them—every producer, every reporter—had a Blackberry and a laptop. And none of them had done the simple search I did? It was two or three days before the rest of the media found him.

I proceeded carefully and respectfully with Neil. When someone confides in her minister, it's confidential. It's like attorney-client privilege and doctor-patient privilege. Under Illinois law, this privilege is perpetual and remains in force even if the client dies. I suspected that applied to "clergy-penitent privilege" as well.

Then again, this was a special case. If Schori told what Stacy confided in him, it might lead to the arrest of the person responsible for her disappearance or death. It might also prevent her killer from striking again.

I didn't hoodwink Neil Schori into revealing the details of his conversations with Stacy. I was patient. I spoke to him several times and created an environment where, little by little, he was able to lead me to all I needed to know—where to look, what to ask.

That first time I met him, I told him, "I understand that Stacy spoke to you in confidence, and that you're reluctant to divulge any details of what she said. But if I ask certain questions and you tell me you can't answer them, then I will be able to draw conclusions from that. Is that agreeable?"

"I could do that," he said.

I said, "Okay. Did Stacy tell you anything about the night Kathleen got killed?"

"I can't talk about that," he said.

In other words: Yes, she did.

"Is there anything that led to Kathleen Savio . . . ?"

"I can't talk about that."

I knew that Neil had left his former church and relocated his ministry because he didn't want to be hounded by a horde of media types.

"I'm not going to tell anybody where you are," I assured him. "So if anybody finds you, it wasn't through me. But I would like to meet with you again."

"Okay, I can do that," he said.

Shortly thereafter, we had dinner at his house with his wife and children. We talked at length. Now I laid it on him.

"You know, Stacy confided in you so that you could tell somebody, because she knew they would believe you. This is the tough part about being somebody in a position of responsibility who's got the information that you possess. You have a balancing act between your profession and your responsibility to a human being who probably isn't alive. You need to put pressure on the state police. At the same time, you've got to conduct yourself so that your credibility is unimpeachable."

We figured out a way to do that, where I could slip out little pieces of information so that they weren't attributed to Neil. Neil could point me in a direction, and I could follow up leads and use other sources. That's something that police do all the time with informants, so you never have to burn them.

I said to Neil, "If the grand jury calls, if you go to the police—"

"I did, but they didn't seem very interested," he said.

I wasn't terribly surprised to hear that, given their lackadaisical handling of Kathleen's death in the first place.

I said, "Well, you didn't quite tell them the specifics of what she said."

Neil started to open up. He told me, "I went over to Drew and Stacy's house once. I was talking to Stacy. Drew left the room and then came back and sort of . . . got behind me, and I had this weird feeling. The hair on the back of my neck was standing up. I had to get out of there. I felt that I was in danger. I vowed to myself that I would never go into a private home again—that I would only meet people at a location that was mutual and public."

He kept opening up to me gradually, revealing information in segments, and I started to put them together.

He told me that Stacy was in fear for her life—that she came to him crying. He tried to comfort her. And she talked about the night that Kathleen Savio died.

Questioned after Kathleen's body was found, Drew Peterson had told detectives that he was home with Stacy the whole night before. Stacy corroborated this.

Three years later, speaking in confidence to Neil Schori, she told a very different story. She said she woke up that night, and Drew was not in the house. She tried calling his cell phone several times. Eventually she got up and went downstairs. She found Drew in the laundry room by the washer and dryer. He was dressed all in black. The clothing he was stuffing into the washer were *women's clothes*.

"Where have you been?" she asked him.

"You know where I've been," he said coldly. "I was taking care of the problem. It'll be the perfect crime."

He instructed her that if anybody asked, he was in bed with her all night. Fearing for her own life, she obeyed, and lied to the investigators.

Now, it's important to note here that this is what's known as "double hearsay"—hearsay within hearsay. Neil was telling me what Stacy told him that Drew had said. Hearsay is generally inadmissible as evidence in a court of law, because it's a statement made by someone not under oath, and thus can't be tested for its truthfulness in court. There are a lot of exceptions to that general rule. Still, you don't want to go to trial with just hearsay as evidence. You want to corroborate.

In this case, Stacy did offer possible corroboration: those calls she said she'd made to Drew's cell phone. There might be records of those calls we, or the ISP, could get our hands on. Obviously, if the records showed that Stacy made those calls, then Drew was not at home with her the night Kathleen died.

"You have to tell the detectives that she said that," I told Neil. "They can get search warrants to seek those records or the phone bill."

We reached out through an intermediary to Stacy's cell phone company, but we weren't able to ascertain if the records existed. I told Neil to tell the detectives that, too.

About a month after I first met him, we convinced Neil that it was necessary to go public on Greta's show. That he owed it to Stacy to keep the pressure on and help move the case against Drew forward. On the show, he spoke about how Stacy called him in August and asked if she could meet with him. Remembering that chilling time in the Peterson household, he arranged for her to meet him in a public place—a Starbucks. He also arranged to have a friend sit nearby to be a witness to the fact that no improprieties were going on. He was, after all, a married man.

This was a huge detail, because that friend could corroborate in court that the meeting took place.

Greta asked Neil what he and Stacy talked about. He said that after some random conversation, "she blurted out the reason" she was meeting with him.

Greta asked, "Which was?"

"She said, 'He did it.'"

"Just like that?" Greta asked.

"Just like that."

Neil wouldn't divulge many details of the conversation on the air—some of which he had already shared with me. He was still sensitive about betraying Stacy's confidence. But he said enough. And a few months later—March 2008—he did the right thing again and testified before a special grand jury convened to consider indicting Drew for Kathleen's murder.

A questionable autopsy report, a newspaper article, something someone lets slip in an interview, or even something he or she doesn't say...these are the details, the minutiae, that gradually build into a case. Most people in the media don't have the training, the inclination, or the time to pursue the small but crucial details. It's one of the things that make my role with FOX different.

For instance, I wanted to find out everything I could about the infamous "blue barrel." The third week of November 2007, the ISP said that on the night of October 28, a neighbor of Peterson's had seen him and an unidentified male haul a blue plastic barrel out of Peterson's house and into his Yukon Denali. Over the ensuing week, Steph and I talked with several sources who identified Drew's helper as his stepbrother, a guy named Thomas Morphey. Gradually, details were added. Morphey said the barrel weighed about 120 lbs. and was warm to the touch. On October 29, he learned that Stacy was missing. He then attempted suicide, swallowing handfuls of Paxil and Xanax, apparently convinced that he'd unwittingly helped his step-brother dispose of his dead wife's remains.

This was not Drew Peterson at his most clever. You ask your stepbrother to come over and help you move a barrel? Why couldn't you take it downstairs by yourself? If he wanted to put something in it, why wouldn't he leave the barrel in the garage and carry the object downstairs to put it in there?

If Stacy was in there, he couldn't just put her in a big plastic bag and haul her downstairs himself. Picking up a limp body is more trouble than it might seem. What if one of your sons comes out of his bedroom while you're doing it?

"Dad, what are you doing?"

"Oh, I'm just taking mommy down to the garage to put her in a barrel, son."

That's a problem. They don't even make a plastic bag big enough. Legs, arms, and everything else would be hanging out and leaking. All kinds of nasty things happen when people die.

Why did he pick Thomas Morphey? Because he had weaknesses Drew could play on. Drew could both threaten and extort him. And after the deed, if Morphey ever spoke out, who would believe him? He was said to be unstable. He'd had a history of DUIs, was once diagnosed manic-depressive, and had done some time in rehab. Two days after they move the barrel, the guy almost overdoses on pills.

When the story did come out, the police fanned out all over the landscape, searching for the blue barrel. The media descended on Morphey like locusts, camping out in front of his home with their microphones and cameras, ready to shout questions at him about his past peccadilloes. I found it loathsome. As usual, they were treating this more like fodder for a Jerry Springer show than news. And it was useless, since all they did was drive Morphey into hiding. He spoke to none of them.

My news producers and I respected his privacy. We left him a note, explaining that we had no interest in his past life, but we were very interested in any facts he could share that might help the investigation.

While police scoured the countryside for the blue barrel right after Morphey's revelations, I went in another direction. If the media were going to paint Morphey as not a very credible witness, then investigators needed to corroborate what they could of his story.

Morphey said that before moving the barrel that night, he and Peterson got coffee. This was a part of his account that could be easily corroborated, as opposed to searching hither and yon for the barrel. If this part of the account proved to be true, it would lend credence to the rest of it. So my news producer, Steph Watts, and I went to three different local spots to try to track down where they had been.

We finally established, by talking to employees, that they had been at the nearby Krispy Kreme the night Morphey claimed they had met. I spoke to the manager. He wasn't unfriendly, but he was very reluctant to talk. The ISP had been to see him and told him not to. He said he couldn't give me the names of the staff who were working on the night of October 28.

"All right," I said. "Can you show me the security camera disks for that night?"

"Oh no," he said. "Corporate wouldn't allow it."

"Come on," I said. "This is a murder investigation. Would corporate want you to withhold evidence?"

Eventually he let me see the tape. I saw two guys sitting in the back. They were too far from the camera for me to make a positive ID. Was it them? I don't know. But if it was—and digital enhancement of the images could probably help determine that—then it was a crucial piece of evidence. It corroborated Morphey's story.

Did the ISP ever ask to see those tapes? Not until I put the word out that they existed, pretty much shaming them into it.

Why was it important to corroborate Morphey's version of events that night? Because it blew holes clean through Drew Peterson's alibi. Drew's version of events was that he worked the late shift the night of

October 27 and didn't get home until 6:00 a.m. Stacy left the house later that morning, October 28, to go visit her grandfather. She never arrived. On the night of October 28, he claimed, she called him from the airport, saying she was leaving him.

While at the Krispy Kreme, Drew left his cell phone on the table with Morphey, and said, "Don't answer that." He then left Morphey alone at the table. Moments later, the phone rang, and Morphey saw Stacy's name flash on the screen of the phone, but he didn't answer it. It was the first of two calls made to establish a phone record corroborating his story that Stacy called him, saying she was leaving him.

Drew insisted he didn't know anything about a blue barrel. He claimed everything Morphey said about the night of October 28 was lies and delusions.

But if a security cam puts them together that night at a specific place and time, and a neighbor testifies to seeing them load the blue barrel into the Denali... Drew Peterson needs a new alibi.

Drew Peterson was uncharacteristically sloppy in how he handled Stacy's murder. He left too many holes. It is my firm conviction it's because he did not plan this murder. I suspect there was a small fight that morning. It didn't have to be a big screaming match or a punch and slug. All Stacy had to do was play the Kathleen Savio card and threaten to tell the authorities he wasn't at home the night Kathleen died.

That's all. She just signed her death warrant. He has to act before she picks up the telephone. She's in the master bedroom. He's got to do it right then.

He's one cold criminal. He has kids in the bedrooms downstairs, and he's killing their mom upstairs.

I met Drew Peterson once, by chance, in late November, 2008. I was crossing the lobby of my hotel when he came in to do an interview with ABC.

"Hey, Fuhrman," he called out, as if we were old friends.

He came over and started talking to me. I pulled him off into one of those little breakfast rooms, and we talked for quite a while, thirty or forty minutes. At a certain point, he went for it. He tried to work me.

"Hey, brother," he said, affecting a posture of kinship. "Why are you doing me so wrong? Come on, man. We're cops."

"No," I said. "You crossed the line. You're no longer a cop."

He laughed.

I kept going. "You're guilty," I said. "You killed Stacy, and you know it."

He was looking at me, saying nothing.

"You probably buried her," I said. "You probably didn't put her in the water. The scuba weights? You're too smart for that."

The scuba weights are an example of everyone focusing on minutiae but getting it wrong. It came out that these weights were missing from Drew Peterson's scuba gear. Everyone presumed that was because he'd used them to weight down the blue barrel when he dumped it in some nearby body of water like the Des Plaines River. The police dispatched divers and started dredging.

I didn't buy it. Drew Peterson's home was excessively neat and orderly. Control-freak, obsessive-*compulsive* neat and orderly. He had to know that any detail that was out of place would be immediately obvious. He knew those missing scuba weights would be noticed. He wanted them to be noticed.

"You could have used ten thousand other things rather than your scuba weights. You knew they would say, 'They're missing. Aha! She

Casey Anthony taking an oath in court.

George and Cindy Anthony could have been spared much anguish if the media hadn't fed the "missing child" delusion when Caylee was clearly deceased.

Haleigh Cummings, whose only crime was being born on the wrong side of the tracks, never got the same level of media attention into her mysterious disappearance. She remains missing.

AP Photo/Mark Carlson

It wasn't until Stacy Peterson went missing that the death of Kathleen Savio, Drew's third wife, was investigated as a homicide. The local media in their community didn't ask questions about her "accidental drowning" in a dry bathtub.

Photo by Peterson family/ZUMA Press

Drew and Stacy Peterson before Stacy went missing. Drew thought he could get away with multiple murders.

AP Photo/The Daily Commercial, C.D. McGonigal

Top: Melinda Duckett killed herself after Nancy Grace harangued her on the air about her missing son.

Bottom: Items police found in the trash behind Melinda's apartment.

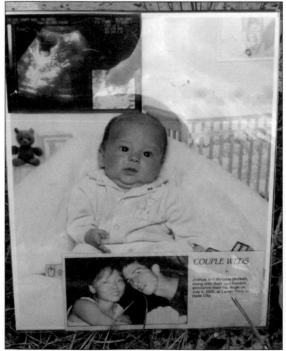

COUPLE WEDS

AP Photo/Leesburg Police Department

Scott and Laci Peterson—before he killed her and dropped her body in the San Francisco Bay.

Michael Skakel thought he had gotten away with murder.

Martha Moxley, tragic victim of adolescent rage.

JonBenét Ramsey's killer was never brought to justice.

John and Patsy Ramsey spoke to the press more than to the police.

Vince Foster, public servant and victim.

Mark Fuhrman wasn't the only detective who found evidence at the scene—but his partner was never called to testify.

Phil Vannatter was in way over his head.

must be in the water.' So while they're looking in the water, they don't look in the ground, do they? And after a winter, they'll never know where the ground was disturbed."

He didn't respond.

I believe they'll never pull Stacy Peterson out of the water. The weights were one of Drew's ways of manipulating the weaknesses of the media and investigators he felt so smugly superior to. Stacy's buried in the ground somewhere, probably not very far from their home. As two, three, and more winters pass, the chances of finding her diminish.

It's an example of how smart Drew Peterson was. Maybe not as smart as he thought he was, but shrewd and clever. He's got a personality. He can really talk—especially to women. He could sell shoulder pads to a snake. But he's also a guy who's in constant denial of who he is. He's got personality disorders they don't have a name for yet.

He played with the media like his personal toys, displaying the Drew Peterson he wanted everyone to see. That's what he was doing every time he said anything to the media. Every single time was a calculated play. He wanted everyone to think, "How could this guy do it? He's good-looking, funny, smart. How could he do it?"

Investigative journalists don't do much investigating. They stand in a pack outside Drew Peterson's house shouting, "Did you kill Kathleen Savio?" I mean honestly, what did they expect him to say?

Little by little, the details and minutiae added up. They pressured law enforcement in Will County to step up, reclassify Kathleen Savio's death, and do a real investigation on Drew Peterson. They blew holes in Peterson's stories about both Kathleen and Stacy.

Not that prosecuting and convicting Peterson would be easy. The ISP and Will County coroner's office had fouled the well with their lackadaisical handling of Kathleen's death back in 2004. Who knows why, but I suspect it goes back to the good-old-boy network. When you've got EMT workers making more astute observations at the crime scene than the detectives, a perfunctory autopsy, and a pro-forma presentation to the coroner's jury by a detective who wasn't central to the investigation, it looks like everyone involved was thinking, "This guy's a cop. I hear he's a good guy. He wouldn't have done this. It must have been an accident." And then, consciously or not, they push the investigation in that direction.

Local media were at fault as well. Where were they in 2004? If I could acquire the autopsy report in 2007 and immediately see problems with it, why didn't they look at it in 2004 and ask the same questions? In 2007, Kathleen's sister Anna showed me and Steph a briefcase filled with documents in Kathleen's handwriting. Journals, notebooks full of entries about abuse and her fearing for her life. Nobody had seen these documents before us—nobody had asked. Okay, maybe it wasn't a national story in 2004, but if you were in local media, and you saw that a Bolingbrook police sergeant's ex-wife died by drowning in a dry bathtub, as the bitter dividing of their assets and the wrangling over custody of their children was taking place, and her family disputes that it was an accident and says she feared for her life and they've got hand-written documents to prove it . . . wouldn't you have looked into that a little? No one did.

Years later, the prosecution on Kathleen Savio's murder case has to interact with that legacy of negligence, indifference, and incompetence. Look at it this way. After Kathleen's body has been decomposing in the grave for three years, it's exhumed. Two pathologists examine it, and both determine it was a homicide. But the original detectives, medical examiner, coroner, and coroner's jury couldn't determine that when the body was fresh. And now that same crew of incompetents is prosecuting Drew Peterson. They didn't know a homicide when the body was right in front of them in the Savio case. Now they're willing to try to prosecute a homicide without a body. I'm not a defense attorney, but even I could win this for Peterson.

Let's imagine Stacy's body isn't found (which it hasn't been as I write this), but there's enough circumstantial evidence to presume she's dead and died at the hands of Drew Peterson. Meanwhile, Kathleen Savio's death has been reclassified as a homicide. Drew goes to jail for that one. The prosecution decides to combine the two cases.

Now, I'm the defense attorney. I've got the lead detective on the Savio case on the witness stand.

"You were one of the lead detectives who investigated Kathleen Savio's death, correct? You determined it to be what?"

"Well . . . I didn't know what it was."

"Okay. But three years after, everybody determines it was a homicide? You didn't know it was a homicide then, but now you do? And you're very eager to prosecute my client for that homicide that you didn't know was a homicide three years ago?

"Now, you have his current wife, who's missing. But you don't have a body. Still, you presume that's a homicide. Even though you don't have a body. Correct?"

"Well . . ."

"Let me get this straight: When you have a body with evidence of homicide, it's an accident. When you don't have a body, you presume it's a homicide. Am I clear about that, detective? You don't need to answer that."

Reasonable doubt, right there. You've impeached the entire Illinois State Police.

In May 2009, a year and a half after Stacy's disappearance renewed interest in Kathleen Savio's death, Drew Peterson was indicted for Kathleen's murder and arrested. He was still joking and hamming it up for the media as he was taken into custody.

As a result of all the attention the Peterson case focused on the incompetent coroner's system, the Will County Board considered a proposal to scrap it and hire a fulltime medical examiner instead. Testifying before the Board, Stacy's sister Cassandra said, "I believe in my heart that had Kathleen Savio's case been properly handled, my sister would most likely be alive today." Opponents of the change—including, surprisingly, state's attorney James Glasgow—argued that it would cost too much. In August 2008, the Board defeated the proposal. The archaic and clearly highly flawed system was left standing, because the county didn't want to pay a medical examiner's salary.

A question has to be asked. How many other Kathleen Savios and Stacy Petersons have there been in Illinois? Or just in Will County alone? How many other cases of "accidental death" in recent years were actually homicides? How many other people died because the murderers remained free to kill again?

Even if Will County does manage to put Drew Peterson away for good, it will be too late for Stacy Peterson.

CHAPTER THREE

WHEN CRIME TV GOES TOO FAR: MELINDA DUCKETT

TELEVISION STARTED OUT AS THE MOST BENIGN and avuncular of all mass media. Clear through to the mid 1980s, it was not a part of television culture to have a host *attack* a guest. Think of the word itself, "guest." That word implies gentility and hospitality.

The word "interrogation" also speaks for itself. But what about when these worlds collide, and crime suspects start coming on TV shows to argue their innocence, while crime TV hosts start to assume the powers and aggressions of prosecutors, lawyers, detectives, or all three? What happens then? You might call this "Gladiatorial TV." It took off in earnest in the last decade, and Nancy Grace is this medium's one woman–super juggernaut.

In 2006, an accident waiting to happen actually happened. Melinda Duckett, the 21-year-old mother of a 2-year-old boy, Trenton Duckett, who had been missing for ten days, was coaxed onto Nancy Grace's show, with the promise that her appearance would help locate her son.

Instead, Grace turned hyper-aggressive on her and, partially through the interview, insinuated Melinda was connected to her son's disappearance. Melinda Duckett went to her grandparents' home and committed suicide. The next day, knowing this had occurred, CNN nevertheless aired the interview. There is a pending wrongful death lawsuit, filed by the family on behalf of the estate of Melinda Duckett, against CNN.

Melinda Duckett's suicide does not mean she was innocent. It does not mean she was guilty. It *does* mean the investigation is ruined, and we'll never know what happened to her child. She remains the prime suspect, and only she was able to help police find the boy.

"The investigators were still substantiating the details given by Melinda of driving around in her silver Mitsubishi Eclipse with Trenton, on Sunday, and visiting family and friends," states the website www.helpfindtrenton.com, hosted by the boy's father, who is still very active in the search. "Melinda had not yet agreed to a polygraph exam. The investigation was hindered tragically, when Melinda took her own life at the home of her grandparents on September 8th, less than two weeks after Trenton was reported missing. To date, investigators are still trying to piece together the timeline for Melinda Duckett between the hours of 5:30 p.m. on August 26 and 8:15 a.m. on August 27th."

The "media" ruined this criminal investigation by going so overboard in their hostility, in pursuit of ratings, that the suspect committed suicide. That is one thing law enforcement is trained to be on the lookout for. We have to have control over our actions and emotions, above all else, or else investigations suffer.

The attorney for the family, Jay Paul Deratany, said in a statement after the family's lawsuit against CNN was filed:

We've alleged that Nancy Grace and her producers deliberately misrepresented the reasons for wanting Melinda on the show. Within minutes of Melinda's phone interview, it became quite obvious that Nancy's questions weren't about finding Trenton at all, but rather about impliedly accusing Melinda of murdering her beloved son.

CNN tried to get the judge to throw the case out, claiming that if it went forward, it would hinder future efforts to use television shows to find missing children. The judge allowed the suit to proceed, overruling CNN's objections.

At twenty-one, Melinda Duckett wasn't anyone's image of a great mom. She still looked like an adolescent. She was emotionally troubled, said to be an "overachiever," and obsessive-compulsive. She gave the impression of being a confused high school student rather than somebody who understands that she is a mother.

Born in South Korea in 1985, she was adopted by an American couple with the surname Eubank at the age of four months. She grew up in New York State, then moved to central Florida north of Orlando as an adolescent to live with her retired adoptive grandparents, Bill and Nancy Eubank. I've never seen details on what prompted that move, but it doesn't suggest a stable, happy family setting.

She met Joshua Duckett when she was a junior in high school. His family background was interesting, too. His father, James Duckett, an ex-Florida cop, has been on Death Row since 1988 for the rape and drowning of an 11-year-old girl.

Melinda became pregnant her senior year, and gave birth to Trenton in August 2004, not long after she graduated. She and Josh had what's called a "tumultuous" relationship. By the spring of 2005, Josh was contacting the police, claiming that Melinda was endangering Trenton's welfare. Melinda was remanded for psychiatric evaluation after police heard a telephone message of her threatening to "end it." Josh later recanted his accusations, saying that his mother, Carla Massero, had put him up to it. That spring, there was an arson fire at Massero's floral shop, where Josh worked. Police questioned two of Melinda's friends without filing charges.

Despite all this, Josh and Melinda were married in July, just short of Trenton's first birthday. But they continued to fight, separate, come back together, and separate again. He alleged that she threatened to hurt and even kill Trenton. They were in and out of child and family services offices. Trenton was passed around like a hot potato, with custody revolving from his mother to his father to his maternal grandmother to the paternal grandparents to a foster family and finally back to Melinda.

In July 2006, a year after the wedding, Melinda filed for divorce and got a protection order against Josh. Her mental and emotional state was apparently deteriorating. She lost her job, applied for welfare, and made some amateur porn videos and photos in her apartment. In one photo, she's leaning naked over Trenton's crib, and in one video, a child is heard crying in the background. According to police, she hacked into Josh's MySpace page and faked a hate-filled message from him to her, threatening that he would kill both her and Trenton.

Shortly after 9:00 p.m. on the night of August 27, 2006, she called police from her apartment in Leesburg to report Trenton missing. He was just a few weeks past his second birthday. She said she'd spent the day with him just driving around and shopping. She said she brought him home, put him to bed in his room, and then had two male friends over to watch a movie with her in the living room. The movie, bizarrely, was *Lock, Stock and Two Smoking Barrels*, Guy Ritchie's violent comedy about a group of bungling amateur criminals. When she went in to check on Trenton after the movie, she said, he was gone and the screen in the window by his bed had been slashed.

Police and the FBI did what you do when a child goes missing. With a missing child, the first days are crucial. They issued an Amber Alert. They searched the area with bloodhounds. They questioned Melinda, Josh, Melinda's two male friends, family, and neighbors. They searched the crime scene and the immediate area.

Searching the dumpsters outside her apartment, they found snapshots of Trenton, his sonogram, and some of his toys in the trash. This gave police a strong indication of Melinda's mindset at the time of Trenton's disappearance, and it was anything but reassuring. She was the primary suspect, and still is.

Investigators determined that Melinda and Trenton were at the Eubanks' house until 4:00 p.m. on August 26, the day before his disappearance. They found witnesses who saw her at 8:00 a.m. and again at 3:00 p.m. on the day he vanished. She was alone both times, even though she told investigators she'd been out driving around and shopping with Trenton all day. Police later said she was frustratingly vague and suspiciously combative when they tried to get a detailed account from her of where she and Trenton went that day.

"She feigned cooperation, but she was uncooperative throughout the investigation," Leesburg police captain Steve Rockefeller said to Orlando TV station WESH. When they pressed her for details, she walked out of an interview. They had to subpoena her cell phone records to try to get some idea of her movements that day. Yet she was very specific in her statements that she and her friends watched the movie together from 7:00 p.m. until 9:00 p.m., and that when she got up to check on Trenton, he was gone.

Here again, if I'm the detective on this case, I am at this point *very* suspicious of this young woman. One red flag with murder suspects is how detailed their memory becomes around the time of their alibi, or, as it were, the time of the murder. The suspect always knows *precisely* where they were and what they were doing when the victim was injured or killed or kidnapped. He or she will be quite adamant about an exact timeframe. That's because it's his or her alibi. And when a suspect—like Melinda Duckett—is oddly squishy and elusive about what she was doing and where she was right before that precise time period for no apparent reason, all your alarms go off.

Melinda continued to dig a hole for herself. Josh passed voice stress and polygraph tests. Melinda took the voice test, and her responses "indicated deception," Rockefeller told WESH. "That was definitely one of the earlier indicators that something was wrong with her story."

Asked to take a polygraph next, Melinda stalled and spoke to the attorney, Kimberly Schulte, who was representing her in her divorce proceedings. Schulte advised her not to submit to the polygraph.

Now, what kind of mother, whose 2-year-old has been abducted, in the terror and panic and whirlwind of activities that follow that abduction, takes the time out to consult a lawyer about how much she should be cooperating with the authorities investigating the kidnapping? And why would she do that? You tell me.

Melinda Duckett wasn't too bright. She was painting a target on herself with her every move. Of course, she was an amateur. She wasn't versed in the ways of law enforcement as, say, Drew Peterson was. But still, she couldn't have worked any harder to make herself a suspect.

On September 7, two weeks into the investigation of Trenton's disappearance, Melinda Duckett was interviewed on Nancy Grace's show by telephone. (The show was taped on September 7, to air on September 8.)

Nancy Grace is a former prosecutor from Georgia. She says she decided to go to law school at age nineteen, after her fiancé was shot to death. As a special prosecutor in Atlanta starting in the late 1980s, she focused on murder, rape, arson, and child molestation cases. Although her aggressive style earned her occasional reprimands, it also won her a 100 percent success rate in getting convictions over nearly a decade.

In the late 1990s, she left the courtroom for Court TV, then CNN. Her fans love her attack-dog style and ultra-tough stance on crime. Her critics despise her for those same qualities. And, just like in the courtroom, her over-the-top style has sometimes gotten her into trouble. She all but convicted the Duke University lacrosse players accused of raping a girl at a party, and didn't apologize later when the accusations proved bogus and charges against them were dropped. When 14-year-old Elizabeth Smart was abducted from her Salt Lake City home, Grace flat-out declared suspect Richard Ricci guilty several times on air. Ricci died in custody, Smart was found, and her abductors turned out to have no connection to the "guilty" man. Grace didn't apologize for that one either, claiming that her critics were trying to "take the police with me on a guilt trip."

Unapologetic, indeed remorseless—Nancy Grace's ratings ensured that she would never be disciplined, and that sooner or later, her going "too far" would cease to be merely infuriating or libelous. It would cross yet a new line, and establish a new low, even by the standards of crime TV.

I'd tell you to go to CNN.com or Youtube to watch the video for yourself, but in the wake of the lawsuit there's no trace of it on the Internet as I write this. You can, however, read the CNN transcript of the program.

Grace starts out treating Duckett somewhat deferentially, as the mother of a missing child. She asks her about the layout of her apartment, where Trenton's bed was in relation to the window with the slashed screen in it, and what time she put Trenton to sleep.

Duckett continues to be very specific about the timeline of these events:

> **GRACE:** OK. Last time you saw him was around 7:00, when you put him to bed. And what time...
> **DUCKETT:** No, that's wrong.
> **GRACE:** OK.
> **DUCKETT:** I put him to bed around 6:30. I'm not sure how technical they're getting, but my friends arrived at 7:00. I checked on him before that.

GRACE: Right. OK. So 6:30, you put him to bed. You went back in to check on him at what time?

DUCKETT: It was before 10 to 7:00 because that's when I got the phone call that they said they were on their way.

GRACE: OK. And when did you realize he was missing?

DUCKETT: It was after the first movie that we had watched. We'd actually planned on two. We went back and we asked them what time we had called the officers, and they said, I believe, it was 9:14. So it was between that time period I'd say…

You see what she's doing here? She's fixing the abduction as taking place precisely between 6:50 p.m. and 9:14 p.m., and then goes on to give her alibi as to what she was doing that whole time—sitting in the living room with two friends. They had corroborated this part of her story to investigators, and also said that they never saw the child while they were in Melinda's apartment that night. Of course they didn't. The child wasn't there.

Grace next spoke to Josh. They discussed his taking the polygraph test. Grace asks him if he has a lawyer, and he says no.

Grace is clearly setting Melinda up for Round Two. She begins to grill her about why she didn't take the polygraph. Melinda turns defensive and combative. She starts sounding like a teenager who thinks she's being wrongfully scolded by an adult.

Grace moves on to Melinda's whereabouts earlier on the day of Trenton's disappearance, and this is when the fireworks start. You can't read it in the transcript, but it's in this exchange that Nancy Grace goes into full Nancy Grace mode, barking her questions and pounding her desk:

GRACE: So where had you been that day?

DUCKETT: We had been all through Lake county and up into Orange.

GRACE: Doing what?

DUCKETT: Basically just shopping, going around driving.

GRACE: Shopping where?

DUCKETT: Well we didn't go anywhere specific.

GRACE: Well I mean if you went shopping you had to go into a store. What store did you go into on Sunday?

DUCKETT: We went throughout the county.

GRACE: Any store? I'm thinking of video cameras, Melinda. I mean maybe they have a picture of someone watching you, following you back out to your car. I mean what store did you go to, Wal-Mart, JCPenney's, what?

DUCKETT: I'm not going to get in any specifics.

GRACE: Why?

DUCKETT: Because I'm not dealing with media very well.

GRACE: Well can you remember where you were that day?

DUCKETT: I can remember perfectly well where I went that day. Just like I have spoken to the FBI with it. But as far as anything else goes we haven't had very good dealings with any of them.

GRACE: Well don't you think it would be a great idea, for instance, if you were at a local JCPenney's or Sears Roebuck, to tell the viewers right now this is where we were. Did you see anything? Did you notice anything? Here's your child's picture? Here's my picture. Help me. Where were you? Why aren't you telling us where you were that day, you were the last person to be seen with him?

DUCKETT: And we have already gone out and distributed the fliers and spoken to—

GRACE: Right, why aren't you telling us and giving us a clear picture of where you were before your son was kidnapped?

DUCKETT: Because I'm not going to put those kind of details out?

GRACE: Why?

DUCKETT: Because I was told not to.

GRACE: Ms. Duckett, you are not telling us for a reason. What is the reason? You refuse to give even the simplest facts of where you were with your son before he went missing. It is day 12.

DUCKETT: (INAUDIBLE) with all media. It's not just there, just all media. Period.

On September 8, the day after the interview, when the show was scheduled to air, Bill and Nancy Eubank found Melinda dead in their bedroom closet. She'd shot herself with Bill's shotgun.

She left several short suicide notes. The notes are printed in large, girlish lettering that looks more like messages scribbled in a high school yearbook than an adult's last communications with the world. She continues to sound like a confused adolescent who feels she's been unfairly criticized:

Your focus came off of my son. I love him and only wanted him safe in my arms. You created rumors and twisted words. Usually I am strong and what others say does not affect me. However I am young, have worked my ass off and still being faced with ridicule and criticism.

She doesn't confess to Trenton's murder or anything so easy as that. Instead, she writes:

The main reason I'm doing this is because after my baby is found, I would not be a good mother. With two jobs and full-time school I tried my hardest, but always slacked in some area. Trenton should of had my full attention at all times. I'm sorry.

———————

CNN heard about Melinda's suicide that day. Nancy Grace was out of town for the weekend, while her producers discussed the matter, and what to do. They decided—against all standards of common decency—to air the show that evening as scheduled.

There was an explosion of media commentary, much of it accusing Grace of having pushed Melinda to commit suicide. In November, the Eubanks filed a wrongful death lawsuit against CNN and Grace. In their lawsuit, the Eubanks claim that CNN

did deliberately make certain promises and representations to Melinda Duckett that appearing on the show might assist in conveying to the public that her child... was missing, which might help in the return of said child, knowing that they intended to surprise Melinda Duckett

> with accusations, questions and verbal assaults clearly
> intending to intimate that she murdered her child. . . .

Well yes, I'm sure they did. Think about it. A producer for Nancy Grace calls you and says, "Hi, we'd like you to appear on Nancy's show. She wants to cross-examine you about why you murdered your child." Would you agree?

Grace, as always, was unapologetic. She insisted Melinda Duckett probably killed herself out of guilt.

Most of the media commentary was about whether it was moral or ethical for Grace to browbeat Melinda Duckett the way she did. From law enforcement's point of view, those are the wrong questions. As far as justice was concerned, what mattered was not whether Grace's actions were unethical but that they were *unhelpful*—detrimental to the case. With Melinda dead, the best hope of finding Trenton, dead *or* alive, was now gone. Nancy Grace hindered an already difficult criminal investigation. If Melinda Duckett didn't do it, but was simply not mentally prepared for the pressure, then the real culprit who kidnapped and probably killed the child is still among us, and has possibly kidnapped or killed other children since. There's a domino effect of unknown consequences.

This is a perfect example of the media's irresponsibility that drives law enforcement up the wall with frustration. The level of stress put on a suspect should be up to law enforcement, not a television program host, even one who's a former prosecutor. The police are monitoring the suspect's movements. If they're going to push a suspect to the point that she might do something drastic, they will have wiretaps or surveillance in place to protect her and the investigation at the same time.

That raises a very important question. Did Nancy Grace's producers call the lead detective on the case and tell him they were going to put Melinda Duckett on the show? Did they say, "Look, this woman's going to come on the show, and Nancy thinks she's guilty. Is there anything that she can ask her for you? Do you have any problems with this? Are we going to interrupt any surveillance? Is she wired, bugged? Is her phone tapped?" Did they give law enforcement the opportunity to respond, "Look, we'd really rather you not have her on until the end of the week. We've got her under surveillance and we're hoping she might lead us to the body, and we don't want her to be spooked."

Or the detective might have said sure, put her on. It can sometimes be helpful to an investigation to have a suspect go in front of the media. TV show hosts don't have to read them their Miranda rights. Anything they blurt out on TV is usable against them in court. If you're dumb enough to say something incriminating on national TV, you're going down.

But I bet Nancy Grace's producers didn't even ask. In my experience, producers of these shows *never* make those kinds of calls. Their primary interest is not in helping law enforcement solve the crime. They're interested in ratings and scooping the other networks. Period. All the claims they make on these shows about justice and crime-stopping are a mockery of the English language.

That's one big difference between the way I operate and the way the rest of the media does. I talk to law enforcement all the time. I see my role as a kind of referee between media and law enforcement. When I'm out on a case, I'll ask the cops, "Anything you don't want us to do or say because it might interfere with your investigation, you let me know. Any place I'm not supposed to be, tell me, and I will steer clear of it. If there's anything you want me to get out in the media to help your investigation, maybe something false to try to stimulate a suspect's movements, let me know, and I'll spin it."

I know the way the detectives are thinking, how they go through a process of elimination and inclusion. I understand what they need to do. I think that's why FOX hired me. I'm the first to admit that they went way out on a limb when they did. What most people in America thought they knew about Mark Fuhrman, what they'd been fed ad nauseam in the media, was that he was a disgraced cop, a perjurer, a racist, and responsible for all the world's troubles, global warming included. FOX took the chance of hiring me, I think, precisely because they wanted some guidance in how to cover law enforcement in the proper way. No other network has a retired detective they actually send into the field to investigate, bring forward information, and advise on what they should or shouldn't do on-air. I've never seen a detective in the field for any other network, nor do I know of one. I don't know why. Skilled, experienced detectives retire every day. All the networks could hire their counterparts to me. And they should.

You might think that as a former prosecutor, Nancy Grace would know the same things I know. But district attorneys are lawyers, not detectives. Most of them have very little knowledge of how an investigation is actually conducted. They don't go out to crime scenes, except maybe for a little show and tell. They don't follow up leads. A detective comes into the office and presents the case to them. Prosecutors are only as good as the detectives who train them.

Nancy Grace's whole *raison d'etre* is she's a staunch supporter of law enforcement. She's TV's toughest district attorney, the special prosecutor in the court of public opinion. And it's true she was a gifted and highly successful prosecutor in her day.

But she's not a prosecutor anymore. She just plays one on TV. And that's very different. When she interrogates a suspect like Melinda Duckett on her show, she's doing it without any of the resources that make for successful interrogations in the real world.

For one thing, there's the setting. You can't properly interrogate a suspect over the telephone or on a TV satellite feed. You interrogate a suspect in the interrogation room at a police station. You're both in the same room. Your face is twelve inches from the suspect's. All the subtleties and nuances of facial expression, body language, and vocal tone come into play.

When you're a detective, you never go into an interrogation unless you know more than the suspect knows. You've done your homework. You're not just blindly firing off questions. Every question you ask is carefully geared to lead the suspect into telling you what you need to crack the case.

Nancy Grace didn't do her homework before she interrogated Melinda Duckett. If she had, she would've known the answers to her questions before she asked them. By asking them, she could have led Duckett away from her evasions toward some kind of useful revelation or confession.

As a TV show host, Nancy Grace didn't have the resources to find those answers. She couldn't send a team of investigators to the malls, for instance, and have them canvass the shops. "Did you see this young woman in here? Did she have a child with her?" However they answer, yes or no, that's useful knowledge. Or there's the movie Duckett watched with her friends. Did she buy it or rent it? Where's the nearest video store? You could check their records and see when she took it out. Then you ask her and listen to how she answers. I guarantee you the police already looked into this. Nancy didn't even need her own investigators. Had she coordinated with the police before the show, they could have fed her useful questions.

"Ms. Duckett, isn't it true you were at the video store at 5:00 p.m. to rent this video? And isn't it true your child wasn't with you? Where was your child?"

Instead, Nancy Grace fired blindly. All she did was work herself into a lather and make Duckett clam up. The next day, Duckett was dead, and the investigation effectively died with her.

Another crucial resource Nancy didn't have was time. When you're a detective interrogating a suspect, you play along, let him commit himself to a story you know is false. You act like you believe it. Sometimes you play dumb. You say, "Well, I've got this other person who says he saw your car *here*." Let him lie again. And you continue to lay out the line. "I've got you on video at an ATM at 9:08 p.m. It shows your face, and your license plate number driving away. Uh, how do you explain that?" You let him explain and pile lie upon lie upon lie. You lead him toward a confession. At some point he can no longer organize the lies, and he starts giving up.

A good detective doesn't lean over a suspect and start right out bullying him. He does the opposite. He tries to come off as anything but threatening. If you're a beat cop in uniform, there are times when you have to be incredibly aggressive and brutal. You always have to maintain a military stance, because you're in uniform, and you don't know when the attack's coming. You cannot let your guard down. When you're a detective, you're humanized, even in the suspect's eyes. You can be more compassionate, gentler. You're not going to kick his ass. And he thinks you're smart just because you wear a suit. You can say, "Hey, look, my boss said go and pick you up, you know. They've got some stuff I need to ask you, a couple things. We can get this done in short order—hey, I see you're wearing a Lakers shirt. You like the Lakers?" Detectives keep candy bars and cigarettes in their desks. I've never smoked a cigarette in my life, but I always had cigarettes to give to suspects. It's surprising how well it works.

You can't use any of those techniques grilling a Melinda Duckett for six minutes between commercials. It takes hours. Sometimes days. You don't even look at your watch.

Time is a luxury TV news people most definitely do not have. They're in a constant rush to beat the clock. They have to have new stories to tell every day. And they have to splice them into carefully timed segments bracketed by commercial breaks. They have to have punchy sound-bites, and they go for the jugular.

Nancy Grace was a great prosecutor. She had skills that earned her a 100 percent conviction rate. But now she's on TV, and she doesn't have the resources or the time to be effective.

Let's be clear. The vast majority of people in the media are not concerned with truth, justice, and the American Way. They're concerned with scooping the other channels. Many of the young producers of these shows don't have the worldliness even to understand the implications of what they do. They're producing shows that cover law enforcement, but they generally know nothing of how law enforcement works. They went to broadcasting school, not the police academy. There's nothing malicious or premeditated in it. They're young, and they're energetic, and they want to go up the chain in the communications field, so they're trying to do what everybody wants.

This all started with the O. J. Simpson case. The media discovered how covering crime can be a low-overhead, massively profitable reality show. They don't have to pay for any actors or backdrops or anything. And it sells like crazy.

But media should be responsible to the case and the victim, because that's really what it's about. It's about the suspect *getting away with murder,* and the media could actually aid him in that if they're not careful. Drew Peterson got way too much face time as far as I'm concerned. The media think they're going to get a confession out of this psychopath? Absolutely not. Meanwhile, Kathleen Savio's family does not come across all that well; they aren't very well-spoken, so they don't get much time on TV.

Media are not and cannot be an arm of law enforcement. I believe Nancy Grace is sincere in her support of law enforcement and her desire to help bring criminals to justice. But Melinda Duckett's suicide is an extreme example of how media actually hinders law enforcement more often than it helps.

With Melinda Duckett's suicide, investigators lost their best chance of finding Trenton. They were reduced to following up on "tips." Tipsters are the bane of investigators' lives. They mostly just make extra work for law enforcement. You have to follow up every tip, no matter how ridiculous. If you don't follow up, the defense is going to have a field day. It means that you made a predetermined decision that this person was the suspect and this child's dead, and you no longer pursued any leads.

It's another very obvious way the media make extra work and distraction for law enforcement, because the media always fan the notion that it's a search for a missing child, and police are following up every lead and tip. They are never going to go on the air and say, "It's been seventy-two hours since this child was reported missing, and we have to begin assuming the kid's dead. In other news…" Their job is to keep that story alive, keep viewers' hopes alive, keep them coming back to see if there have been any new breaks in the Caylee Anthony story or the Trenton Duckett story. In Caylee's case, it was obvious the minute the child's hairs were found in the wheel well of the trunk of that car that Caylee had come to a bad end. From that moment on, it's not a search for a missing child, it's a murder investigation. But if they say that on the news, the story's over. So day after day, week after week, the media keep up the pretense.

In this case, campers in the Ocala National Forest—a huge park very near Leesburg—said they might have seen Melinda and Trenton in the woods on August 27. Police combed the entire area, sent divers into the lake there, and even planned to trap some of the lake's alligators to examine the contents of their stomachs. Nothing turned up. And while all those law enforcement personnel were engaged in that useless operation, they weren't getting other work done.

No trace of Trenton has yet been found as I write this. Is he dead? I think the chances are ninety-nine to one he is. Did Melinda do it? I'd say that's highly likely. Now, thanks to Nancy Grace, we'll probably never know.

CHAPTER FOUR

MURDER AND THE UPPER CLASS: MARTHA MOXLEY

IN 2002, MICHAEL SKAKEL WAS CONVICTED of the 1975 murder of Martha Moxley, and given twenty years to life.

Look at those dates again. It took twenty-seven years for justice to be served in the Moxley case. Twenty-seven years during which local law enforcement and local media seemed to do everything humanly possible *not* to catch the pretty 15-year-old's killer. In fact, I'm confident that Michael Skakel would still be a free man today had not a lot of outside pressure been brought to bear. Dorthy Moxley would still go to bed every night not knowing who killed her daughter.

My interest in the case was first sparked by my late friend Dominick Dunne, whose 1993 novel *A Season in Purgatory*, a fictionalized account of the murder, threw a very unwelcome spotlight on what was by then an ice cold case. Four years later, I went to Greenwich, Connecticut, to do my own research. The investigation my associate

Stephen Weeks and I did led to the publication of my book *Murder in Greenwich* in 1998. One month after my book appeared, Connecticut convened a grand jury to reexamine the case. Thus began a process that eventually led to Michael Skakel's conviction.

I'm not Monk or Sherlock Holmes. I did nothing thousands of other competent detectives, or ex-detectives like me, would not have done. Yet what I did was what should have been done, right from the start—and probably would have been done, if Martha Moxley hadn't had the misfortune to be bludgeoned to death in one of the wealthiest enclaves in the country—Greenwich, Connecticut. But fortunately for her, I investigate the same way regardless of the status of the victim, suspect, and/or their family connections in society.

If you think the rich and powerful don't get to live by other rules than you and I do, this chapter might change your mind.

Some of the material will be familiar to you if you read *Murder in Greenwich*. But I wrote that more than a decade ago, well before Michael Skakel's trial and conviction, and before I had the media experience I now have. I didn't quite realize it at the time, and I'm sure the reporters didn't, but the way the media covered Martha Moxley's murder is another prime example of journalists simply following the leads they're handed, instead of looking at facts and trying to draw their own conclusions—never mind create their own leads. So much for the "watchdog" media.

Had the media asked the right questions and persevered despite the stonewalling, foot-dragging, and cover-up that protected a rich and powerful family, they could have kept the pressure on law enforcement to solve a case they were obviously reluctant even to pursue. And it wouldn't have taken the snooping of an outsider and *twenty-seven years* for justice to finally be served.

I have never in my life been treated more shabbily than I was in Greenwich, CT. And that includes the Simpson trial. From the minute Stephen and I arrived, we were treated not just like unwanted outsiders, but like pariahs. Everybody in Greenwich thought they knew who I was and why I was there, and they weren't happy about it. They knew I was going to turn over some rocks they'd been content to leave unturned for two decades. They knew or at least guessed what kind of slimy secrets were under those rocks. They would much prefer it all stay hidden.

The prevailing attitude was that what happened to Martha Moxley was a terrible tragedy, but it was a long time ago. Greenwich had moved on, the Moxleys had moved out, and that case was never going to get solved. The murderer had surely been an outsider, probably some black guy from the big city. He was never going to be found. The only reason Mark Fuhrman had come to their town was to try to dig up dirt for his next bestseller, and they weren't about to lift a finger to help. With a couple of exceptions, everyone from the cops to the coffee shop guy clammed up around us, except to try to insult me. People didn't answer when we knocked on the door. In one case, they called the cops on us just for knocking. The triumphant headline in the next day's local paper, *Greenwich Time*, said it all:

GREENWICH SLAMS DOOR ON FUHRMAN
FUHRMAN FOILED IN BOOK RESEARCH

That attitude spoke volumes about a fundamental lack of human decency. No one cared that a young girl had been murdered in their community and the killer was still free. All they cared about was keeping their quiet, privileged lives undisturbed. Residents circled their wagons to protect their way of life, and the cops and local media, who knew which side their bread was buttered on, followed suit. It was simply cowardice and politics—people not wanting to stir the pot.

Greenwich, CT, is a close-knit community, a small town of about 60,000, and one of the wealthiest towns in America. It's less than forty-five minutes by commuter rail from Grand Central Station, making it a kind of far-flung suburb for Wall Street financiers and other captains of New York industry. Belle Haven, where the Moxleys lived and Martha died, is Greenwich's most exclusive neighborhood, a peninsula where forty huge mansions sit on vast, manicured estates. Private security guards patrol its streets and check out anyone trying to enter. It is a small, safe center of power and privilege, where everyone knows everyone else, houses are left unlocked, and keys are left in cars.

Brutal murders are extremely rare in Greenwich. In fact, at the time of Martha Moxley's death in 1975, local law enforcement hadn't conducted a murder investigation since 1949. Not only were they inexperienced, they also had effectively no training in it. It just didn't come up. There might be a suicide every now and then—retired detective Steve Carroll, one of the few people in Greenwich who was cooperative with me, told me he investigated two during his years on the force. But otherwise, the life of a Greenwich cop was as quiet and uneventful as the lives of the city's wealthy residents.

The Greenwich police department was about as hostile and uncooperative with me as they could be. They knew how poorly they'd handled the Moxley investigation, and they sure didn't want me writing a book about it. One of the first things Steve and I did was to go to the police station and ask for a copy of the released Moxley case files, which, after twenty years, added up to some five hundred pages. While we sat and waited, an older, uniformed officer walked by. He was a captain. He turned back to me and said, "There's nothing new in those reports."

"Well, I'm new," I said.

He just rolled his eyes.

When we got the files, we saw they'd been heavily redacted. Lots of black lines were scrawled throughout text on the pages. The thing about redacted documents is that even what somebody chooses to censor tells you something. If they're disturbed enough about something to redact it, that's a point you should look into. It's another example of what people *don't* tell you being more useful than what they do. What are they hiding? Why? Whose name is it they've blocked out? Why don't they want other people to talk to this person? Maybe that's someone worth contacting.

I was stonewalled by the state attorney's office as well. I went to Greenwich hoping to cooperate with the police and prosecutors. If they'd help me do my research, I'd give them any useful information I turned up. It's how I try to work with law enforcement on every case I investigate. I figured we all wanted to close this long-standing case and bring the murderer to justice. It wasn't long before I realized that hope was naïve.

In 1975, the Moxley family were newcomers to Belle Haven. Originally Midwesterners, they'd moved east from California in 1974 so that David Moxley could run the Manhattan office of the big accounting firm Touche Ross. They were outsiders in the close-knit, guarded neighborhood, but they were rich (of course), white, and good people, and they had little trouble settling in. Their neighbor, Rushton Skakel, sponsored their membership in the ultra-exclusive Belle Haven Country Club; their teenage kids Martha and John fit right in at school.

The Skakels were Old Greenwich, as well as being Kennedy relatives. Rushton was the brother of Ethel Kennedy, RFK's widow. He'd inherited running the family business, the giant corporation Great Lakes Carbon. Like the Kennedys, they were a big, somewhat unruly Catholic family—six boys and a girl. When his wife Anne died of cancer in 1973, Rushton sank into alcoholism and often left the kids with tutors and other caretakers while he traveled, drank, and pursued women. With their father away so much, the kids ran free, and two of the middle sons, Thomas, who was seventeen when the murder happened, and Michael, fifteen, ran wild. They drank, partied, liked to pull mean pranks, and were both prone to violent bursts of temper. Tommy was outgoing and popular, and enjoyed bullying his quieter little brother. They often came to blows.

Dorthy Moxley, like some other mothers in Belle Haven, worried about Martha being around the Skakel boys. But Martha was fifteen and growing into a true beauty. She apparently enjoyed flirting with both brothers.

In Greenwich, October 30 is Hacker's Night, when the parents and police look the other way while teens run a bit wild and get into mischief—mostly just innocent Halloween pranks and loud parties. But on Hacker's Night 1975, the mischief turned deadly.

Martha went to a party at the Skakel house. The kids, as usual, had the run of the place. Rushton Skakel was out of town. A new tutor, Ken Littleton, had just started work that day as a live-in guardian, and hadn't had time to exert much control over the household. Martha was sitting with Michael when Tommy, asserting himself over his little brother as he often did, horned in. Michael drove off with friends, and as the party broke up, some kids saw Tommy making out with Martha outside the house. Afterward, Martha walked toward home.

She never made it. Dorthy, her mother, waited up, worried, and eventually fell asleep on a couch. The next morning she called around to neighbors, and even walked over to the Skakels' house and asked Michael if he knew where her daughter was.

Martha's body was found in her own backyard a little past noon, under a pine tree, in a huge pool of blood. She had been viciously bludgeoned about the head with a golf club. Her attacker had struck her with such force that the club, a six iron from a rare Tony Penna set, shattered in several pieces. As the *coup de grace*, he shoved one piece, the handle and lower part of the shaft, straight through her neck.

Trails of blood leading across the lawn to the scene indicated that Martha was first attacked some distance away, near the front of her house, in a spot that was open to view and partly lighted by a streetlamp. From there, she had apparently been dragged, still alive, across the Moxley's gravel driveway to a more secluded spot on the lawn, where she was beaten more. She lay there, near death, perhaps for thirty minutes, before the attacker, or someone else, returned and dragged her to the final, more hidden spot under the pine tree, where her murder was concluded.

The complete inexperience of the Greenwich police showed immediately in their mishandling of the crime scene. I'm still a cop at heart and don't like to slam other cops, but the bungling here was unconscionable.

The procedures for handling an outdoor crime scene are well-established. The first officers to arrive at the scene have four clear responsibilities: determine if the victim is dead or alive; establish whether the perpetrator is still on the scene; protect the scene and all evidence on the scene; and start a log.

The two officers who were the first to arrive botched these basic steps comprehensively. One of them actually couldn't stand the sight of blood and panicked. Over the next ninety minutes, the crime scene was overrun by a horde of officers, detectives, doctors, journalists, and neighbors. No one was in control of the scene or the investigation. The victim's body, the most important piece of evidence at every murder scene, was handled and moved by a dozen people before being taken away. Other evidence was contaminated, tampered with, or just lost. One officer actually allowed a dog to lick up some of the trail of blood in the leaves and grass. A dog literally ate evidence! A state police crime lab was eventually called in. They didn't arrive until nightfall, did some cursory work, and left soon after. For all the crowds and activity, very little evidence was actually collected, and most of it was useless.

This was another glaring example in which you don't need to be an ace detective to read the crime scene and see where the clues pointed. I could read it clearly more than twenty years later. Martha Moxley's murder was a rage killing. The killer struck her so viciously that he shattered a six iron, then drove part of it clear through her neck. That's a pretty obvious indication that he had some relationship to her. Which, in a closed community like Belle Haven, means he was probably a neighbor. Who among the neighbors had a relationship with Martha? Well, the Skakel boys. They both had histories of violent outbursts of temper, as local law enforcement well knew. The murderer used a rare type of golf club. Who in the neighborhood owned a set of Tony Penna clubs? As it turned out, the only set in Belle Haven was in the Skakel house. They belonged to the late Anne Skakel. Since her death, the boys were often seen knocking balls around with them on their lawn.

Hm, you think we should get a search warrant for the Skakel house? Separate all the kids who were at the party and interrogate them individually?

This should have been a three-day case.

But the cops didn't do that—because this was Greenwich, and because it was the Skakels.

In Greenwich, the police are like a civil service security force. The wealthy residents they serve tell them what to do and when to do it. The cops are their employees—literally. A lot of the cops on the force had worked off-duty for Rushton Skakel, doing private security, chauffeuring the family around, parking cars at parties, or running errands. The higher-ups on the force came over for dinner and drinks. I was shocked at how chummy they all were. If you didn't want to solve Martha Moxley's murder, because you were pretty sure a Skakel had done it, these were the guys to handle the investigation.

———————

The police did stroll over to the Skakel house. They didn't take a search warrant. They just asked if they could look around and were given permission.

This was more bad police procedure. When someone lets you search their house without a warrant, they can also stop the search at any time. The minute you reach for the drawer where they have hidden the evidence, they can say, "Okay, stop. I changed my mind. Get out." And you have to go.

Still, they did find Anne Skakel's golf clubs in the house. And the six iron was missing.

Was it the shattered club found near Martha's body? They couldn't determine that with certainty, because a curious thing happened with the evidence at the scene. One piece of the shattered club wasn't recovered—the handle and lower part of the shaft. Coincidentally, this was where Anne Skakel's name was printed on all her clubs.

This is how I knew somebody was trying to cover up for the Skakels.

When the first two officers arrived at the body, they saw that piece of the shaft sticking through the girl's neck. Not long after that, it had *disappeared.* Either somebody relatively early on the scene pulled it out of her, or it was accidentally dislodged and somebody picked it up.

Either way, that somebody made it disappear. In the official report, it was simply missing.

The Greenwich police knew that missing piece was important. They searched in ponds, they searched in yards—all over the place. But oddly, they forgot to talk to the two officers who were the first ones at the scene. Nobody in the police department talked to them. None of the reporters covering the case ever spoke to them either. Nobody talked to them until Stephen and I did, twenty-odd years later. We called them simultaneously, to prevent them from conferring with each other on what they said. Steve called one, while I spoke to the other. They both said the shaft was still in her neck when they got there—which implicated everyone on the scene but those two cops.

"Why didn't you speak up about this?" I asked the one I spoke with. "Why didn't you tell anybody?"

"Nobody asked me," he said.

"When your department was searching for this missing part of the shaft, didn't you think you should say something?"

"If somebody asked me, I would have told them."

Nobody asked, because nobody wanted to hear the answer. That missing piece was never found. Somebody, most likely somebody on the force, did a favor that day not just for the Skakels, but for everybody in law enforcement and the media who didn't want to go up against the Skakels. That's why that missing piece of the golf club was so important. Not because it was needed to identify Martha Moxley's killer—it wasn't. It was important because the very fact that it had gone missing showed how compromised the investigation was right from the start, and how law enforcement's responsibility to truth and justice, and the media's responsibility to telling the whole story, gave way under the influence of wealth and privilege.

———————

While the cops couldn't *not* look at the Skakel boys, they could certainly not look too hard. Tommy was interviewed that day, and said he'd last seen Martha heading for home around 9:30 p.m. He passed a rudimentary polygraph test a few days later. He would continue to be the brother investigators were most interested in, to the extent that they were interested at all. Michael had a solid alibi: he was away with his friends until about 11:30 p.m., when he came home and went straight to bed. Since the cops believed the murder occurred between

9:35 p.m. and 10:00 p.m., they gave Michael a pass, and his name doesn't surface much in their files after that. In fact, it's no exaggeration to say that he wasn't a suspect until I came along more than two decades after the fact.

The family stopped cooperating with investigators a few months after the murder. As the months turned into years, and the 1970s bled into the 1980s, the cops wasted a lot of time looking busy and getting nowhere. They identified and interrogated a ludicrous grab bag of "suspects," many of whom didn't have a ghost of a connection to the case. In my book I listed more than forty, male and female, some of them as far away as New York City. All they had in common was that none of them could be placed with Martha Moxley the night of the murder, and none of them was a Skakel.

Closer to home, Ken Littleton, the Skakel's new tutor, came in for a lot of scrutiny, despite the fact that he also had no connection to Martha, wasn't seen with her that night, and had no credible motive for bludgeoning her to death. In truth, he was just a convenient fall guy, and the state made his life hell for several years when they should have been focusing on the Skakels.

Even after Michael was convicted and sentenced, his cousin Robert Kennedy Jr. kept insisting that Littleton was the more likely suspect. In a long article in the *Atlantic Monthly* in 2003 called "A Miscarriage of Justice," he argued that his cousin was innocent, said I'd just been fishing for my next bestseller, and accused Dominick Dunne of leading "a *Lord of the Flies* frenzy to lynch the fat kid." He claimed that "the state's case against Littleton was much stronger than any case against Michael Skakel."

This was as wrong in 2003 as it had been in the 1970s.

What were local media doing as the lackadaisical investigation dragged on through the 1980s? Were they putting pressure on the law, raising questions about the ineptitude and the appearance of a cover-up, pursuing their own leads, and demanding that justice be served?

In a word: No. For the most part, they just wrote articles based on press releases and statements from the police. A couple of local reporters pushed a little. In the early 1980s, Len Levitt of *Greenwich Time* discovered that Greenwich police had made almost no records from the Moxley case available to the public. He got the paper to submit a Freedom of Information Act to have the files released. What the cops coughed up was heavily redacted, but still helpful. However, Levitt's bosses, the owners of the paper, shelved his article in 1983. It wouldn't run until 1991, when the William Kennedy Smith rape case in Florida indirectly brought renewed attention to the by-then very old Moxley case and the Kennedys' relatives in Belle Haven. (It was this same family connection that prompted Dunne to begin the research that resulted in his 1993 book.) Unfortunately, Levitt was convinced that Tommy, not Michael, was the murderer.

Of course, *Greenwich Time* wasn't the *New York Times*. It was basically a glorified community newspaper. Its writers weren't much in the business of "investigative journalism," a term in vogue in those years immediately after Watergate (and one I'm pretty skeptical about). Its editors and owners weren't much in the business of making life uncomfortable for their wealthy subscribers or their advertisers.

The pathetic truth is that the only people who never gave up hope and never stopped demanding justice through all the years of nonactivity were Dorthy and David Moxley—and, after David died in 1988, Dorthy alone. Long after they moved out of Greenwich, they kept offering rewards and trying to keep the pressure up to find the person who put their daughter in a Greenwich graveyard.

But no one else seemed to care. That's why, over twenty years later, I found myself following leads no one else had pursued, talking to people like those two cops whom no one had talked to before, and asking questions no one else had asked.

Another side-effect of the William Kennedy Smith case in 1991 was that Greenwich and the State of Connecticut felt pressured to announce that the Moxley case would be "reinvestigated." Over the next few years, this new effort proved to be as bungling and fruitless as the original investigation. But it did have the effect of prompting Rushton Skakel to hire a New York detective agency, Sutton Associates, to do a private reinvestigation for the family. It was an exercise in damage control. Tommy and Michael's dad wanted to know how much was out there implicating one or both of his boys.

It turned out there was a lot. After a lengthy investigation, Sutton hired a young writer to create a report. This young man secretly fed a copy to Dominick Dunne. Dominick saw it was dynamite, but he didn't know what to do with the information. I think it was so explosive that he was also afraid of it. He was a good writer, but not a trained investigator. So he passed it along to me. The minute I read it, I said, "Michael did it."

The Sutton report contained a lot of information on Tommy and Michael's behavior and statements after 1975 that had not been made public. They were both very troubled young men, substance abusers, drifting through life, clearly conflicted about...something. But Michael was the more damaged. In the years following Martha's murder, he was in and out of trouble with the law, in and out of reform school, in and out of various rehab facilities and institutions. He once joked about a girl with a golf club sticking in her chest, and another time allegedly confessed to the murder of Martha Moxley during a group therapy session.

Most damning was that in interviews with Sutton investigators, Tommy and Michael gave very different stories about their activities on the night Martha Moxley was killed than they had twenty years earlier. Tommy now admitted that he and Martha had been together longer than he originally stated, and that their necking ended with mutual masturbation. If this was true, it pretty well eliminated him as a suspect. A teenage boy is highly unlikely to fly into a homicidal rage at the pretty neighbor girl who just brought him to orgasm.

But what about his unstable, picked-on younger brother and rival for that girl's affections? If he came home after several hours of sulking to discover that the two of them had sex, might he fly into a drunken, jealous rage?

In his 1995 interview with Sutton, Michael completely changed his original alibi. He admitted lying to the police in 1975. He now said that when he got home around 11:30 p.m., he didn't go straight to bed. He went back out and walked over to a neighbor's house, where he said he often peeped in a window to see the woman of the house walk around in the nude. From there, he said, he went over to the Moxleys' and climbed a tree outside a window he believed was Martha's room. He called her name a few times, and when she didn't respond, he took out his penis and masturbated to orgasm. He then walked around to the front of the house, where the streetlamp was, then to the area where Martha's body was eventually found, before returning home.

Why did he so radically change his story after twenty years? Why was his new one so bizarre and embarrassing? And why was he now going out of his way to place himself at or near the crime scene around the time of the murder?

Remember: The suspect always has a detailed story to tell about where he was and what he was doing when the crime took place. I believe that, given the new interest in and reinvestigation of the case, Michael Skakel feared that the truth was finally closing in on him. He needed a new alibi that placed him outside at the time of Martha's murder, in case any new witnesses turned up to testify that they'd seen him. He felt the new alibi had to be so strange and embarrassing that it'd be believed. Who'd make up a story about window-peeping and masturbating in a tree?

I was convinced Michael was Martha Moxley's killer. In my book I offered a hypothesis of how it went down. When he came home that night, he probably saw Tommy and Martha together, then saw Martha leaving for her home. He flew into a jealous fit and followed her, carrying one of his mother's clubs. He confronted Martha near the front of her house, there was an angry exchange, and in a burst of rage he struck her with his mother's golf club. Then he dragged her a short distance, away from the streetlamp, and beat her some more.

He then hurried away from her, but did not go home. He lingered outside, panicked and shocked at what he'd done. Eventually he decided he couldn't leave her lying where she was. He returned and dragged her to the more secluded spot under the pine tree. Seeing that she was still, incredibly, clinging to life, his rage welled up again. He beat her savagely and stabbed her through the neck, finally killing her. Then he snuck back to his house.

To me, this was the likeliest version of the night's tragic events, based on the evidence and simple common sense. It didn't make any sense that Tommy killed Martha, or that Ken Littleton killed Martha, or that some shadowy stranger from out of town with no relationship to her killed Martha. Any detective would have gone through the same process of elimination that I did and focused on Michael.

As long as that detective didn't work for the Greenwich Police Department and the Skakels.

My book was published in the spring of 1998. The grand jury was convened a month later. Michael was arrested in January 2000, and went to trial for murder in 2002. He was forty-one, bloated and balding. The prosecution's version of the murder was more or less what I described in my book. Several witnesses testified that Michael had confessed or even bragged about killing Martha over the years, including one occasion when he was said to have boasted, "I am going to get away with murder. I am a Kennedy." His defense attorneys took a simple approach, trying to bolster his alibi and cast doubt on the prosecution's witnesses.

He was found guilty in 2002. Rushton Skakel died the following year. Michael's appeal for a new trial was turned down in 2007.

———————

The Martha Moxley story was made-to-order for an enterprising journalist. It was a long-unsolved murder mystery in a place where murder mysteries never happened. It had wealthy and powerful people in it, and connections to the Kennedys. It was about privilege and influence, clear incompetence, and possibly corruption and a cover-up. It had all sorts of loose ends to track down. What journalist wouldn't want to take it on in those Woodward and Bernstein years?

But the media in Greenwich, just like law enforcement, were compromised and conflicted. If you want to be Woodward and Bernstein, you've got to go at it 100 percent, at the possible expense of your job, your future, and maybe your health and your family's well-being. You've got to have the courage to risk it all, and above all, you've got to be responsible to the truth. The journalists and the detectives in this case were not responsible to the truth. Somebody who's worried about getting fired if he does the right thing isn't going to do the right thing.

When I went to Greenwich, I wasn't a cop or a detective anymore. My face was known to everybody. I was not a popular guy. Yet I was still able to get information and get people to talk to me; still able to put things together and deduce the truth. I didn't need to be a genius or Columbo or the Profiler. It just took experience, common sense, and an unbiased eye. That's all it required to help move the ball to the point where Martha Moxley's murderer was eventually put behind bars.

What could a journalist have done in my place, with the power and money and connections of a newspaper behind him? How long would it have taken for Michael Skakel to be arrested and charged? A few weeks, a few months, a year?

Everybody dropped the ball, for almost three decades, because nobody really wanted to know the truth. Nobody except for the Moxleys.

CHAPTER FIVE

PORTRAIT OF A MAMA'S BOY: SCOTT PETERSON

I **WILL NEVER UNDERSTAND WHY MURDERS HAPPEN**, no matter how many times I have to look into the eyes of a man who killed everything that mattered in his life.

And for what?

In the case of Scott Peterson, fertilizer salesman and pathological narcissist, it was probably an accident. Probably a fight that escalated. Probably a moment when his pregnant wife Laci confronted him with what he could not stand to see about himself—the evidence that he was so shallow and rotten that he cheated on his wife when she was carrying their first child. She probably discovered that he was having an affair with Amber Frey, around whom he had also spun a web of lies, telling her he had "lost" his wife. Maybe Laci got hold of his cell phone. Or intercepted emails. She would have confronted him, probably fairly upset. He would have had to kill her, rather than look at himself in the mirror she was holding up.

Laci Peterson's murder gripped and horrified the nation. A pregnant woman, all the way back to the ancient Greeks, is the central symbol of vulnerability. And an eight-month pregnant woman is particularly vulnerable. She can't run, she can't move too fast. The only thing she can rely on and hope for is that her pregnant state will protect her. After all, who would kill a pregnant woman? Who would kill his own wife, eight months pregnant with *his* own child?

Scott Peterson is a classic figure—a Mama's boy. He looks like a man on the outside, but he is still a boy on the inside. Mommy always took care of everything, and he never developed discipline or character. This is one of the most dangerous archetypes in our society. These guys never, *ever* admit wrong-doing, no matter what. They're spoiled and self-centered. When a Mama's boy does something wrong, he just hides it under the bed. He breaks a glass as a kid—he hides it. He just gets rid of it. *I didn't do it.* I didn't eat that cookie. I didn't break that vase. I didn't do this and I didn't do that. Mommy will clean it up. It's never my fault. Somebody else is supposed to protect me from whatever feelings *made* me do it. That somebody is Mommy. This attitude has afflicted Scott Peterson's whole generation. They were never tested by fire because they never had to be. There was always somebody rescuing them.

I had to kill her, he says to himself. But she deserved it. I am the one that matters. I am the *only one* that matters. And now I will hide even this under the bed, hide it from the world, hide it from myself. To guys like this, people have value only when they want to use them. The women they're with are possessions—and those women have to reinforce what isn't there to begin with: their sense of manhood. If they don't, they're wrong. When women in relationships with these men inadvertently challenge their sense of masculinity, it starts tripping the rage. Maintaining the relationship becomes a bigger and bigger problem for the suspect.

These guys—Scott Peterson and Drew Peterson being two prime examples—function fine, but something is broken in their heads. They start out getting into little scrapes. They verbally abuse women, slap them around maybe. Then there's a moment when they go too far, and they kill. Something snaps. It's not intentional murder, it just happens. Then you have the cover-up. And the cover-up becomes the story, not the homicide. We don't know how Laci Peterson died. We'll never know. A mama's boy will never, ever confess.

So persuasive are Mama's boys' denials that they pull otherwise rational people into their web of nonsensical insanity—brainwashing them until they, too, can't see the elephant in the room. To this day, and to my amazement, there is an entire online community, around the world, devoted to the idea that Scott Peterson is innocent and that this case was a terrible miscarriage of justice. I will relieve you of that anxiety by the end of this chapter.

Scott Peterson killed his wife and his unborn son. Evidence doesn't lie. Mama's boys do.

There they were: a strikingly good-looking, young Modesto, California, couple, weeks away from the birth of their first child. They knew he was a boy, and they named him Connor. Laci had put the finishing touches on the nursery—decorated with nautical themes because Scott loved the water—and was smiling brightly in all the last photos taken of her. Her due date was February 10, 2003, just six weeks away.

The families of Scott and Laci were tight-knit, looking forward to spending Christmas together, and all anticipating the birth of the new baby.

It's December 24, 2002. Christmas Eve. Here is where the curtain goes up, in each and every murder that is presented to the American public via the media. The play begins at the end, in a sense, when the curtain lifts on Act One. The Mystery. The big question mark. Somebody is missing. The story doesn't develop "legs" if the victim is found murdered; they should be *missing* first, so the tension can be built up in the audience. What is going to happen? Act One casts a spotlight on the scene just before darkness falls, and it is a scene of perfect, middle class normality.

In this case, Act One has Scott Peterson, on Christmas Eve, in the early afternoon, returning from a "fishing trip" in Berkeley's Marina to find his pregnant wife Laci missing, with her cell phone and pocketbook left behind.

This, already, is troubling. Why would he freak out just because Laci wasn't home? Maybe she went for a walk. At 2:15 p.m., while he was allegedly heading home from his fishing trip, he left a message on her cell phone that started with the words "Hey beautiful..." Detectives later learned that, as all her friends and family knew, her cellphone battery was dead, and had been for several weeks. But that voicemail was his attempt to stop the clock and create an alibi. We see it all the time. A murderer has a small window of time when every second is self-conscious and documented, like no normal hour in our lives ever is. Often, this period of time shows up as one the suspect is sensitive to, and trying to distance himself from the victim as he accounts for his movements. Detectives are on the watch for stories in which the details become absurdly meticulous, as they did in Melinda Duckett's and Michael Skakel's alibis. The signs in this case that something was amiss were very obvious, and present from the first moment.

Laci had last been seen in their Modesto neighborhood that day, December 24. Her mother had spoken to her the night before, and she'd made no mention of Scott going on a fishing trip the next day. Laci didn't know he even owned a boat. He told somebody else that he had made plans to go golfing that day, not fishing.

First of all, why was this man *fishing* on Christmas Eve? Here is what he wanted investigators to believe: that on Christmas Eve, with an eight-months-pregnant wife, he decided to drive ninety miles to Berkeley Marina, to spend *twenty minutes* fishing for sturgeon, a kind of fish he had never fished for before, in a low tide, at the wrong time of day (allowing him only those twenty minutes to fish), and using the wrong tackle. We had a FOX producer make this drive and talk to the fishermen at the harbor. Even a non-fisherman knows that you only go fishing in the right tide, when the fish are biting, which is something that you *inquire* about. But Scott Peterson, having driven ninety miles on Christmas Eve, supposedly went fishing for twenty minutes, in a boat his wife never even knew he owned, and using equipment that you couldn't catch a large steelhead with, never mind a sturgeon. This got laughs from the fishing experts we consulted.

It gets stranger still. He goes back to the house, finds Laci missing, and suddenly decides to start mopping the floors and doing laundry. The first cops to arrive found mops and buckets outside the house. The first uniformed officer to the house knew immediately that it was not a missing person case. He knew it as soon as he saw all the cleaning materials, as well as Scott's demeanor. He called the detective who would be put in charge of the case and said so. Her likely fate was obvious to all the detectives, and they immediately began handling the case as a homicide. The lead detective who was called was so convinced he drove straight back from his vacation, in Lake Tahoe. Only the media couldn't—or didn't—read the obvious signs, and began the drumbeat that Laci was "missing."

The maid said she had mopped the floors of the entire house the day before, on December 23. Scott said Laci had been mopping, and he decided to put the mop and bucket outside the house.

Why?

These are the kinds of elephants you can parade right through the media, untouched. They won't take the hammer and hit the nail on the head with it. Their device is to say, well *maybe*. Anything is possible, when you're trying to stretch your ratings as far as possible, and keep "questions" open that are an insult to any human intelligence.

In Scott Peterson's case, *maybe* he decided to go fishing for sturgeon for twenty minutes on Christmas Eve, in low tide, with the wrong tackle, having driven ninety miles, and then maybe he decided to mop the floors and do laundry when he returned, after reporting his wife missing. There's about a one in a billion chance of such strange behavior not being suspicious.

When I was interviewed about the case, reporters would sometimes say to me: "But they had no real evidence. They put a guy on death row just because they didn't like him."

This is another example of how inexperienced and downright clueless the media can be about crime. There was plenty of evidence against Scott Peterson, and most of it came from his own mouth. Lying to Laci about having several mistresses and about owning a boat was just the start. He lied to Amber Frey, lied about what he was fishing for on Christmas Eve, and kept on telling lie after lie at his trial. The guy is a *pathological* liar.

None of his responses or behaviors—none—suggested he was innocent. They ranged from strange to incredibly bizarre to blood-chillingly insensitive.

The day after Laci disappeared, Scott hosted a turkey dinner at the couple's house in Modesto. A turkey dinner, because, after all, it was Christmas Day. Only a psychopath would believe that this behavior would make him seem normal and innocent. His pregnant wife went missing the day before, and he's cooking a turkey? But in Scott Peterson's twisted mind, this act was supposed to convince everyone he was blameless. He insistently invited next-door neighbor Karen Servas, who'd found Laci's dog, McKenzie, running loose in the neighborhood the day before. She declined, citing her vegetarianism, which prompted him to call her back a second time and tell her he was also cooking tortellini. He sounded calm and cool, she said. She was persuaded, and came over to find Scott's parents, Jackie and Lee, "very upset," while Scott was whistling in the kitchen, acting like nothing had happened.

He told another one of his lies during that bizarre dinner: he claimed that he'd volunteered to take a polygraph test, but police had urged him not to because he was too emotional still. In fact, police had repeatedly urged him to take the polygraph, but he refused.

Servas testified that the look in Scott's eyes that night was so chilling she bolted out of the house, and was spooked enough to flee her home and stay with friends.

A close friend of Laci's, named Stacey Boyers, also visited Scott on Christmas Day, and reported that he spent an inordinate amount of time vacuuming around the couch, armchairs, washer, and dryer. Again—does this make any sense whatsoever, for an innocent, worried-sick husband? No. He was still cleaning up evidence.

As police searched for Laci during the following days, Peterson's bizarre behavior continued. When an officer named Chris Boyer, who ran the bloodhound tracking team, told Scott he wanted to take a pink slipper, a hairbrush, and a pair of Laci's sunglasses to track her scent, Mr. Wonderful demanded a *receipt* for the objects. Boyer was shocked speechless. He said that in twenty years in the field, nobody had ever asked for a receipt for objects that could help locate a missing person.

Being a psychopath and narcissist, Peterson seemed blissfully unaware that he was only making everyone very suspicious of him. He thought he was God's gift to the world. And, like Drew Peterson, he thought he was smarter than everyone else—that he'd pulled off the perfect murder. But as soon as he told police about his Christmas Eve "fishing trip," they started to search the Marina.

By the first week of January, Amber Frey had already contacted the police and agreed to tape her telephone conversations with Peterson. He'd lied to her the whole time she was seeing him. She thought he was a widower. He didn't admit to her that he was married until January 6—by which time she was already, without his knowledge, cooperating with law enforcement.

Once investigators began to wiretap him and keep him under surveillance, there were several instances where his behavior simply shouted out his guilt. Each time there was a lead on a possible Laci sighting, he dismissed it, looked bored, snorted disdain, or laughed. He deleted a message, with a laugh, from his mother, talking about new information in the search, when he didn't know he was under surveillance. Once, when an object retrieved from the Bay was found not to be Laci's body, but something else, he said, "Phew." When Laci had been gone for sixteen days and friends asked about hopeful leads in the search, he said coldly, "I bet they'll never find her."

In late January, Frey went public about her affair with Scott. He went on TV a few days later to claim that he'd told Laci about the affair, and that it wasn't anything she'd leave him over. Really? You tell your pregnant wife that you're sleeping with someone else and she shrugs it off?

On April 14, the body of a woman and a male fetus washed up a few miles from where Peterson had claimed to be fishing on Christmas Eve. Police arrested Peterson four days later, pulling him over in a '94 Mercedes-Benz. On him, they found his brother's driver's license, $15,000 in cash, several credit cards (some belonging to other family members), maps of California, a bottle of Viagra, and sleeping pills.

Peterson's trial began in the spring of 2004 and lasted until November, when the jury found him guilty of the murders of both his wife and his unborn son.

Scott Peterson wasn't convicted on his lies and bizarre behavior alone. There was compelling forensic evidence. For one thing, a neighbor saw him load a large object shaped like a human body wrapped in a plastic tarp into his car on the morning of December 24. His explanation? He was transporting patio umbrellas to his storage space. On Christmas Eve? Later, a large plastic tarp washed up in the Bay, with duct tape attached to it.

A hair of Laci's, confirmed by mitochondrial DNA, was found in a pair of pliers on his boat—a boat Laci never even knew he owned, which he had purchased only weeks earlier. The fact that a hair manages to lodge itself onto a pair of pliers inside a boat that Scott owned and Lacy never knew existed is very powerful, but is even more powerful because the hair was found on an item in the boat that was most probably used to prepare Lacy to be dumped in the San Francisco Bay.

Remember Caylee Anthony's hairs found in the wheel well in the trunk of the car? This is no different. How many times did the child ride in the trunk? How many times did Laci Peterson use the pliers in the boat she did not ever sit in or even know about? At Peterson's trial, the defense claimed that Laci was in the warehouse where the boat was stored and used the bathroom there—in other words, she must have seen the boat there and known it was Scott's. That's still a far cry from her getting inside it, finding the pliers, and using them to pull out her hair.

There were blood spots on a comforter in the house, and the blood was identified as Scott's. He said he cut himself all the time at work. But how did the blood get on the comforter in the bedroom?

Also incriminating were five cement anchors he owned. He could not locate four of them when investigators asked where they were. The obvious presumption is that he used them to weigh down the body.

Like Drew Peterson, another psycho narcissist, Scott Peterson basked in the media spotlight and tried to play them for his own purposes. And the media played along. They made his relationship with Amber Frey the centerpiece of the story, rather than the overwhelming evidence against him, mounting each day. They made the story cloudy, emotional, and for Peterson, easy to handle. He could just talk about his regret over cheating on his wife.

The pinnacle moment came when Peterson was interviewed by Diane Sawyer in January 2003.

Why did he do it? Why did he agree to be interviewed by Diane Sawyer? Actually, it was a mutually beneficial deal. Both of them are deeply invested in ratings.

TV hosts are controllable, and murder suspects know it. Their goal is to use the big TV hosts to sell their case to the jury pool. They know everyone watching them is a potential juror. That's why they do it.

Meanwhile, for the host, there's always tomorrow. Another show, another murder. While they care about the outcome, their lives are not invested in it. They're not responsible for solving the crime. They're trying to get ratings. Scott Peterson, Drew Peterson, and O. J. Simpson all believed that they could charm and convince their way out of trouble. Specifically, they all thought that they could charm *any* woman.

This was as tough as the Diane Sawyer interview got for Scott Peterson. Tilting her head and wincing slightly, in that way she does when troubled, she said, "I think everybody at home wants the answer to the same question: Did you murder your wife?"

He's on national television, watched by millions. Did she think he was going to say *yes*?

Peterson, playing his role just as expertly as Sawyer played hers, replied:

> No. No, I did not. And I had absolutely nothing to do with her disappearance. And you use the word murder and right now every one is looking for a body. And that is the hardest thing because that is not a possible resolution for us. To use the word murder and—yes, and that is a possibility. It's not one we're ready to accept and it creeps in my mind late at night and early in the morning and during the day all we can think about is the right resolution to find her.

This statement is a perfect example of saying too much, when a simple "no" would suffice. By overstating his case, it's clear Peterson was trying to convince not only Diane Sawyer, but everybody watching—and perhaps even himself—that he had nothing to do with the murder he committed.

Peterson probably chose Diane Sawyer because she's pretty and charming, so he felt comfortable. He also knew what to expect. Television hosts and anchors have an on air persona that their audience anticipates. Unfortunately, suspects routinely choose their hosts and shows specifically because they know exactly what to expect, and how to manipulate the content.

When I was watching this interview, I became very frustrated. These TV hosts have somebody in their hands, and they unknowingly let them slip away because they don't really understand how to go about it.

In an interrogation, it's very different. The key moment in an interrogation, when the suspect is ripe to give that one little tidbit that will actually be so unexplainable, it will ultimately indict him in front of twelve people—you don't botch that.

The media are not willing to see that opportunity and take it, because they're concerned about the performance, finishing the interview, filling the time. But you mustn't miss that key moment. You see the suspect is vulnerable; you have to know when to go in, and what to say when you do. And that means you have to have a plan. And the plan can't be written down on a piece of paper, like all of these media people do. Producers give them questions, they do research, but it's all way too linear and flat.

As even a former prosecutor like Nancy Grace has shown, media people just don't know how to interrogate a suspect. They ask questions that go nowhere and mean nothing. Worse, they can actually help the suspect build up sympathy.

Diane Sawyer had him, but she didn't push it. She didn't ask him, "How did Laci's hair get in your boat? When was she in it? Where are the four concrete anchors?" Not a single person in the media, whether it's Larry King, Diane Sawyer, Matt Lauer, or anybody else, looks at a suspect in a situation like this, as a detective would. It isn't their fault—it's their circumstance.

A detective approaches a suspect with a pace and methodology according to the information he has. In the end, if you think he is going to sidestep the question and invoke an attorney, you are not above confronting him—calling him a murderer.

A detective could use any of the following statements if he feels he is starting to lose the interrogation: "Look, I'm gonna tell you something. I think you're a murdering scumbag. I think you killed your wife. I think you're so stupid and so delusional that you're thinking that this story actually holds water. Who do you think you are to try to flim-flam, the entire country, on top of killing your wife and throwing her in San Francisco Bay?"

Why is it so important to be confrontational with the suspect? Because you want to see the suspect's reaction. It means you've reached a point in the interrogation when you realize this guy's not going to give it up. He's not going to commit to things. What you do then is try to get under his skin. You switch tactics, from being a sympathetic, meek detective to being a lion in a cage. You point your finger and go, "You know something? You're just a *coward*. You couldn't kill a man, you have to kill *women*. You're just a little boy, that's what you are. You have to pick on women because you weren't man enough to pick on a man."

You do this because you have a last-ditch opportunity. You go for it. You have a captive audience—until he asks for an attorney. When you sense he's on the verge of doing that, you pounce. Sometimes you break them, sometimes you don't.

However, most hosts won't say these things. They could—they have a prime opportunity to get the suspect to react—but the network attorneys won't allow it. Unfortunately, to get an interview with a suspect, there are usually agreements that certain questions will or won't be asked, to keep the suspect from saying certain things. TV interviewers are constrained by network fear of legal repercussions. Stations, concerned with ratings, don't want to alienate anyone who supports the suspect, or prevent the suspect from coming on the show again. Their legal department says, "Well, he's just a person of interest." There's always that disclaimer. But there's no box on a crime report that says "person of interest." There's "victim," "witness," and "suspect." However, the media are petrified that if they flat-out call some guy a suspect on the air, they'll get sued. Do they really think Scott Peterson is going to sue ABC, and then be deposed under oath as part of that lawsuit and have to answer questions that he wouldn't otherwise answer? Somebody you *know* murdered their wife is going to sue you?

It takes a cop about five to ten years, if he's really paying attention, to understand how to deal with people in an interrogation. You have to pay attention on the street. You have to watch older cops, you have to watch detectives, you have to understand how to get into a suspect's mind a bit and break down his natural defenses.

TV hosts are the same in every interview. Everybody's got a consistent on-air approach. However, that's the last thing you want.

A suspect can't be able to predict your body language, tempo, or style, or else he's going to have an easier time lying to you.

Detectives have a *bag* of personalities. In a classic interrogation, two detectives will team up for this role-playing. One might say, "Look, you know something? I'm too close to this, I'll tell you. And I apologize for this, because the victim looks a lot like my sister. And I'm gonna tell you, I really, I apologize, but I think I'm being unfair to you. I'm gonna let my partner ask you these questions, because you know something? I don't even think you did it."

Now the suspect thinks, "Okay, I flim-flammed that guy, he's an idiot."

The partner comes in and says, "I have to tell you, I'm not as experienced as my partner, but I gotta ask some questions because I've gotta fill in these boxes on this report because, you know, we gotta get this done. I have to ask you some questions. Some of them might be sensitive and they may be accusatory. That doesn't mean I think you did anything, but I got to ask them because we have to move on. I hope you understand, sir. Hey, do you want a Coke or something? I'm getting a cup of coffee. I'll get you one. What do you want in it?"

The suspect now feels these two detectives are either idiots or they don't believe he's killed anybody. You can actually see the tension in his body relax by the way he's sitting. And then you sit back too. You don't sit forward, you don't sit up on your elbows, you sit back, you cross your legs.

"You know something? I'm just gonna take notes when I think I need to, but you know, I think this is gonna be pretty quick."

All you're doing is getting him to commit to one lie, or one truth. He knows when he killed his wife or girlfriend. The only thing you need to commit him to is that period of time. You go back to it, you go forward, you go back to it again, and as the session progresses, you unfurl facts that he doesn't know you know. You have to have these ready.

As I noted about Nancy Grace's bungled interview with Melinda Duckett, having those facts at hand makes all the difference. Imagine if Diane Sawyer's producers had put a timeline chart of Scott Peterson's activities on the screen, and then she'd said:

"Mr. Peterson, look at this timeline. I want to ask you a question. Does it seem reasonable to you that somebody on Christmas Eve, with close family on both sides and a pregnant wife, on *Christmas Eve*, his first Christmas with her carrying his child, would drive ninety miles to *go fishing*?"

Then she could show a taped interview with the harbor master, saying that the tide was wrong. And an expert fisherman, laughing at Peterson's fishing equipment.

"Mr. Peterson, do you really think that's reasonable?"

I'd have loved to see him lie his way out of that on national television. Then she could have done the same with his sudden burst of cleaning when he got home that day.

"Mr. Peterson, we talked to your wife's mother, who said you're kind of one of those sports slobs. The last time you did laundry you were probably in college. So did you turn OCD just this day? You just decided to mop up the floor and start doing laundry? Let me see, your wife is missing, you don't know where she is, you're frantic, you're calling family members, and then, 'Oh, I got to go put in the laundry. Yeah, I think I'll do a little mopping too.'

"Mr. Peterson, what I think you were doing was cleaning up a crime scene and cleaning up the clothes you were wearing when you committed that crime."

But her hands are tied. Meanwhile, an opportunity for justice is lost, while the suspect's chance to create sympathy is realized. The media thinks they're covering a murder, while the suspect is using them to run a public relations campaign.

They don't realize it, but in the media, the show trumps the victim. In law enforcement, the victim trumps everything else. The media have to start caring about the best interests of the victim—before it's too late for our society.

I always contend that there are very few premeditated murders between people who know each other, unless it involves business and money.

This was clearly not a premeditated murder. Who would plan to kill his pregnant wife on Christmas Eve, with family coming over the next day? Scott Peterson killed Laci out of impulse, probably the night of December 23.

Then he had to dispose of the body. He had to either cut her up or bend her up, put her in a cooler, put her in the back of the truck, drive ninety miles to San Francisco Bay, put his boat in the water, put the cooler in there, get out there, spend twenty minutes dumping her body, and then come back, put the boat on, and drive back.

He figured out what he needed to do to explain his actions at the time of her disposal. She had talked to her mother at a certain time the previous night. The clothes she was wearing the previous day, when she was last seen, were not found at the house. That means they were on her, which means she probably never went to bed that night.

Here is where he constructed his alibi. The murderer always has an alibi. But you can't make up the natural progression of life in your head without making a mistake. You're trying to make it too perfect, trying to answer too many questions. If you were to ask me where was I last Wednesday, I'd have to say, "I don't know." When detectives first heard Scott Peterson's account of where he was and what he was doing when Laci went missing—which was both really precise and really strange—I'm sure they began to have their suspicions right away. Scott Peterson lied his way straight to death row.

Before 1994, there were no reality shows except for *Cops*. Now it's like we're watching fish in a bowl. That's our entertainment. That's what the O. J. Simpson case did to our culture.

It's cheap. There are no producers, no directors, no budget, all the actors are free, and all the participants and locations are free. Everything is free. They discovered this during the Simpson trial, and that's how reality TV was unexpectedly born.

Once Simpson started doing interviews, attorneys and suspects realized—hey, I can take my case to the people. Suspects try to manipulate the truth. They're not going to testify in court. What they're doing is testifying to what they want to say without having anybody cross-examine them. It might be the only place that you see the suspect talk about the crime—on TV.

The media should reach out to the investigators and ask, "What might I ask that might help you?" It's unfortunate that media people don't realize how distasteful law enforcement finds them. Or they just don't care. There's a responsible way to report crime, by respecting and including law enforcement. They should put the death of the victim first, and the ratings second. But it's the other way around.

And now there's no going back.

The prosecution of Scott Peterson cost the Stanislaus County taxpayers $4.13 million. Meanwhile, it *earned* hundreds of millions—an incalculable amount—for the mass media.

Scott Peterson was found guilty of first degree murder in the death of his wife, and of second degree murder in the death of his unborn son—the double conviction made possible by a new law passed in 2004 called "Connor's Law." He was sentenced to death. At his sentencing, Laci's mother enacted the voices of both Laci and his unborn son, pleading for their lives. Scott showed no emotion at all. His father stormed out of the courtroom, screaming that the members of Laci's family were all "liars."

In the summer of 2009, Peterson's family, their resources totally drained, sent out a fund-raising plea to his supporters, for their next planned appeal, asking for donations of between $5 and $50.

Peterson sends letters from prison about his defense, and his innocence, that go up on a blog for his supporters to read. The tone is sterile and dull. He blames the media for everything. Mama's Boy is still getting all kinds of attention, all kinds of help. He has learned nothing. He has simply gotten more skillful at snowing people, even fellow inmates, whom he works on convincing, one by one, insisting that he "loved" Laci.

Nothing is his fault, still.

And it never will be.

The lesson to women is: learn to spot a sociopathic, narcissistic Mama's Boy before he spots you. Sometimes, as a detective, I think the best thing we could do for women is teach them who not to fall for.

CHAPTER SIX

DEATH OF A TROUBLED PRINCESS: JONBENÉT RAMSEY

IN THE RATINGS-OBSESSED MEDIA CULTURE, the brutal murder on the night of Christmas Day, 1996, of 6-year-old pageant princess Jon-Benét Ramsey was the perfect story to kick up the notoriously slow holiday news cycle. In turn, it became a national obsession almost on par with the JFK assassination. It has shattered careers, set off a minor avalanche of lawsuits, cost taxpayers untold millions of dollars, and haunted the American psyche. Despite years of maniacal scrutiny by the media and debate over every shred of evidence, people continue to be sharply divided about what it all points to. Some people believe an intruder broke into the Ramseys' house and murdered the Ramseys' little girl. Others maintain the Ramseys did it. The case has become a "whodunit" of epic proportions and has created an Internet subculture that continues to live and breathe all things JonBenét, all the time. Because it's officially "unsolved," it's still a cash cow for media poised to exploit every new "break" in the case, like John Mark Karr's delusional confession in 2006. Tragically, media involvement in this case destroyed lives and has practically ensured that JonBenét's killer would never be identified.

———————————

Seen with a detective's eyes, the case is not that complicated. But just like in the JFK case, it started to *seem* really complicated, especially as the media hurricane intensified. Once you muddy the waters, pretty soon you can't recognize the really stellar facts. You question *everything.*

I will grant this: it was a very bizarre and unusual case, and the evidence was, in many instances, strangely opaque. Both possibilities—that the Ramseys did it and that they didn't—strained the imagination. I don't think anybody is an idiot for believing in the intruder theory. But I do think those who do probably don't work in law enforcement.

I became involved in the case by way of a phone call I got from Steve Thomas, whose career at the Boulder Police Department (BPD) was destroyed by the case, and who I believe was and is the only committed advocate the victim—JonBenét Ramsey—ever had. Steve called me in the spring of 1997 because he was distraught and wanted my advice. He had established his career in narcotics, and had a 13-year unblemished record as a detective. However, he was assigned to the Ramsey case when it was two days old.

Steve resigned in disgust from the BPD on August 6, 1998, after nineteen months of backbreaking work on the case, which was thwarted and obstructed at every turn by deference to the Ramseys. The special treatment they were conferred was due to politics, power, and an abiding refusal to treat these suspects as *suspects*. John Ramsey was a powerful figure in the business community in Boulder—and his connections certainly didn't help the investigation.

If you think I am partaking in a "witch hunt" when I say that, tell me of a single other murder investigation where the central suspects are not interviewed formally by police for *two months* after the murder, because one of them is too distraught and "in no shape" for such a thing.

Somehow, though, the Ramseys weren't too distraught to give interviews to the media, or hold press conferences which conveniently allowed them to get their message out to potential jurors without having to deal with a police rebuttal.

The more details of a case that get leaked, without police review, to the public, the harder it is for police to bring a killer to justice. Suspects can talk to the media. The police can't. The smallest piece of evidence could be crucial to an investigation. If kept secret, finding out whether a suspect knows about it can either convict or exonerate him or her. If exposed to the world, it adds material for the cranks and false tipsters who inevitably flood high-profile cases with leads the police have to follow up—leaving less time for real investigative work.

"What I witnessed for two years of my life was so fundamentally flawed, it reduced me to tears," Thomas wrote in his $8\frac{1}{2}$-page, detailed, and very damning letter of resignation from the BPD.

> During the investigation detectives would discover, collect, and bring evidence to the district attorney's office, only to have it summarily dismissed or rationalized as insignificant. The most elementary of investigative efforts, such as obtaining telephone and credit card

records were not met with support, search warrants denied. The significant opinions of national experts were casually dismissed or ignored by the district attorney's office, even the experienced FBI were waved aside .... In a departure from protocol, police reports, physical evidence, and investigative information was shared with the Ramsey defense attorneys, all of this in the district attorney's office "spirit of cooperation".... I was advised not to speak to certain witnesses, and all but dissuaded from pursuing particular investigative efforts. Polygraphs were acceptable for some subjects, but others seemed immune from such requests. Innocent people were not "cleared" publicly or otherwise, even when it was unmistakably the right thing to do, as reputations and lives were destroyed.

Over the course of the investigation, at least fifteen lawsuits were filed from all parties in all directions—against the Ramseys and by the Ramseys—seven of which were libel suits. Lawsuits were filed against the tabloids by the Ramseys...against the BPD by former detectives...against the Ramseys by people named as suspects, for ruining their lives. One was even filed by the housekeeper, whom Patsy implicated. The pattern you see in these lawsuits is that the ones filed against the Ramseys went nowhere. Summary judgment, usually. But the Ramseys' lawsuits tended to be successful, resulting in handsome settlements, including one against a tabloid and the *New York Post*, and one against the publisher of the book written by Steve Thomas about the case.

You may know the ins and outs of the case like the back of your hand. But in case you don't, let's review the final hours of JonBenét's short life:

On December 25, after the children had opened their gifts, the Ramsey family attended a Christmas dinner at 5:00 p.m. at the home of friends, a couple with the last name of White (who have also filed a few libel suits). The Whites were fairly new friends, wealthy like the Ramseys, with children of similar ages. The Ramseys left that dinner party at around 9:00 p.m., dropped off presents for some friends, then arrived home at 9:30 p.m. They say JonBenét was fast asleep in the car, that John carried her upstairs and put her in her bed, left the room, and that Patsy then removed JonBenét's black velour pants and put long johns on her, leaving her in the same white top she had worn to the party. Both Ramseys maintain that John left the room when Patsy changed her daughter's pants and put a pair of long johns on her. Both Ramseys maintain JonBenét never woke up, did not brush her teeth, and did not eat anything before she fell asleep (after arriving home).

At 5:30 a.m. the next morning, Patsy said she woke up, and inexplicably decided not to shower. She put on her makeup and the same outfit she had worn the night before, a red sweater and black pants.

Then she descended the stairs, where she came upon a 2 $^1/_2$-page, handwritten ransom note, screamed for her husband, and ran to JonBenét's room. JonBenét was gone, and she asked her husband, hysterically, "What should I do?" (Odd choice of words—what should *I* do—but these are her words from the police interview.) "Call the police," he said. He went, supposedly, to check on their 9-year-old son Burke, and found him still sleeping.

The story is not quite right at every single juncture, starting right here. Why would such a corporate alpha male like John Ramsey not have taken charge in this very moment? Why did he ask his wife to call the police if she was clearly helpless? They remember everything a little too perfectly, down to the timing, whereas most people in a stress situation don't remember what they said or how things happened. They may even contradict their story as they piece it together after the fact—that is, if they're innocent.

Patsy called 911 and breathlessly reported that her daughter had been kidnapped and gave the bare essentials of the ransom note, which is one of the longest, strangest ransom notes in history. The note (written, as it was later discovered, on paper from a pad found on the kitchen counter, using a sharpie pen found in a cup next to it) was filled with bizarre rants, claimed the kidnappers were part of a "small foreign faction," and demanded the very low, odd amount of $118,000, which matched John Ramsey's 1996 bonus from his company. It also threatened that JonBenét would be instantly "executed" if the Ramseys contacted any authorities before handing over the money, and said they were under constant surveillance. It said that the Ramseys would be contacted by phone the next day between the hours of 10:00 a.m. and noon. It also threatened to "behead" JonBenét.

To radically simplify a narrative that has been bogged down by infinite minutiae, here is what happened next: Officer Linda Arndt arrived, friends the Ramseys had called arrived, and Burke was taken to the White residence. Arndt was simultaneously trying to calm, interview, and, apparently, keep the Ramseys at home during the next several hours. She was also trying to secure the crime scene, though it was not yet a "crime" scene.

It was widely observed and reported that John and Patsy Ramsey seemed totally disconnected from each other on this day. They didn't speak, make eye contact, or comfort one another. The house became a strange brew of shadow-plays, all arranged around Patsy Ramsey's understandable hysteria and John's strange remoteness.

For some unfathomable reason, neither Arndt nor any other of the law enforcement officials in and out of the house that morning thought to check the house. Instead, Arndt asked *John Ramsey* to do so, with his friend Fleet White. "See if you find anything unusual," she said. This would be the second time the two men would make their rounds.

The two men had not been looking for long when the case took an extremely dramatic turn. Around 1:30 p.m., John Ramsey went into a dark room in the basement (which had already been hastily checked by his friend Fleet earlier) and yelled, "Oh my God!" JonBenét was lying there, wrapped in a blanket, garroted, with ligature around her neck and wrists, her arms flung over her head, bent to one side, and black tape over her mouth. Her father ripped the tape off her mouth and carried her up the stairs, where everybody was screaming for ambulances and the like, though it was clear that the child was in full rigor mortis. John Ramsey placed her on the floor, and she was confirmed dead. Patsy Ramsey burst from the restraining arms of her friends in the sunroom where they'd been waiting and fell upon her daughter's body, wailing and screaming for Jesus to raise her from the dead. A priest who was in the house started reciting last rites.

The murder victim was then moved for a second time by Linda Arndt, who inexplicably felt she should be placed near the Christmas tree. She placed a sweatshirt over the body. It was 2:00 p.m. before the house was declared a crime scene. The Ramseys left the house and went to stay with friends. They never returned to the house where Jon-Benét was killed.

Due to the holiday, the coroner did not arrive until 8:00 p.m., and JonBenét's body was not removed from the house until 9:45 p.m.

The crime scene was hopelessly contaminated, due to the fact that by the time it was known to be a crime scene, countless people were traipsing through the house, the victim was moved twice, carried by one suspect and embraced by the other, whose fibers and DNA were now all over the body.

As she subsequently revealed, Linda Arndt knew John Ramsey was involved. She said, as Ramsey recounted in *The Death of Innocence*, that she counted her ammo to see if she could defend all the people in the house against a possible attack from John Ramsey before reinforcement arrived. Arndt was the only law enforcement officer in the house when JonBenét's body was found and for way too many hours after that. You can see that hysteria in different forms overtook the scene from the outset. And it remained that way. Arndt wound up, like so many people on this case, imploding from anger, paranoia, and hostility, filing a lawsuit against the City of Boulder and her former employers, claiming they used her as a scapegoat and destroyed her reputation, and that she knew who the killer was.

I imagine Steve Thomas was brought in because Arndt seemed troublesome, or too emotional, or too anti-Ramsey. But Steve Thomas himself would eventually be reduced to weeping, devastation, and resignation, after a year and a half on the case.

Suffice it to say, something was, from the outset, very wrong, and even depraved, about this investigation. I can't prove who killed Jon-Benét Ramsey, but I can tell you who the evidence points to. I also can speak to the investigation—what was normal versus what happened—and tell you this is the most absurd police investigation I've ever witnessed into a homicide.

When I spoke to Steve for the first time, about three or four months into the investigation, he opened up to me and told me a lot of what was going on, which was really a story about what *wasn't* going on, and how frustrated he was. The first thing he said was, "How do I deal with the media?"

"That's easy," I told him, "you don't."

The media had descended on the normally peaceful town of Boulder and were hindering detectives' work to an alarming degree. They offered money to anyone potentially connected to the case for information they could turn around and sell to their addicted audience. They printed rumors about the investigation that damaged already-tense relations between the Ramseys and the police department, and crucial confidential information that could help identify a killer was splashed in headlines across the nation.

Exacerbating their problems as well was the totally incompetent DA's office, which overturned heaven and earth to find JonBenét's killer, unless that killer had the last name Ramsey. They got involved in the police investigation when they should have stayed out of it.

Thomas told me, to my amazement, that he was blocked by the DA's office from conducting his investigation. He was never allowed to use search warrants to get the Ramsey's financial and phone records. We're talking real basics here—Standard Operating Procedure

(SOP). Normally, within twenty-four hours of a murder, a detective gets search warrants anywhere he needs them—financial records and phone records that include cell lines, home and business landlines, and business lines. Steve wasn't able to get any of that.

If you're in charge of a homicide, once the scene is done, and you have interviewed the people you need to interview initially, you split people up, you interview them *separately* and *immediately.* You record them, surreptitiously or out front, however you have to do it, and you get an initial story, timeline, and commitment from them. That's very important. It lays a foundation. The further things move from the event, the easier it becomes for the suspects to get their lies organized, and synchronize their stories, and you don't want that to happen, because it can doom the investigation if they get the upper hand. It becomes much harder to interrogate them.

Most homicides, due to this swift standard operation protocol, are solved within the first seventy-two hours. But most murder suspects are not affluent and well-connected, like the Ramseys. Consequently, Steve was unable to interview the Ramseys separately for *two months* after the murders. That is unheard of.

In Los Angeles, there's one person in charge of a murder investigation, and it's the lead detective. Nobody decides for him if he should or should not get a search warrant. He writes a search warrant and takes it to the judge. He doesn't say, "Boss, can I do this?" That's absurd. We don't have to ask if we can interrogate or even arrest somebody. We are trusted to do what we need to do.

But the Ramsey case was different. It was never spoken outright, yet it was clear. People in a community who are elected or appointed, or can be fired at will, will ingratiate themselves with those in power. They all go to thousand-dollar-a-plate dinners together and in a split second it is made clear that this or that detective has to go. Ramsey doesn't have to say a word.

Steve was a problem. He would not go along with the program, and the program was to let all kinds of things go and essentially let the Ramseys dictate the investigation.

I told Steve, "You know they're going to pull you off this case, right?"

He said, "Yes, I do. I can feel it."

I said, "Make copies of everything. You have a loyalty to the victim only, and not to those pinheads who are running the town in Boulder."

He did. And that enabled him to later write his exposé *JonBenét: Inside the Ramsey Murder Investigation.* Steve became convinced that Patsy Ramsey had killed JonBenét, in a rage over bedwetting, possibly in the bathroom, and he said so not only in his book, but on *Larry King Live* to the Ramseys' faces. The Ramseys sued for libel. His publisher wanted to settle, but Steve refused. By then he was working as a contractor, which he does to this day. He said, "I'll sell everything I own to defend this book. I want no part of any settlement." Leaving him out of it, his publisher settled with the Ramseys, while he held onto what was most important to him—his voice. While Steve was temporarily gagged due to the lawsuit, I was on TV a lot talking about the case, and I became his champion in the media, speaking for him when he could not.

We had many long conversations about the case. I remember a few highlights that have since become common knowledge to JonBenét watchers.

Many people believe an intruder came through a window in the basement of the Ramsey house, leaving a scuff mark. John Ramsey had broken the window the previous summer when he was locked out, and they had never had it fixed. However, the evidence contradicts this theory—and you must always follow the evidence.

"Mark," Steve told me when he called me in distress, "nobody came through that window. There were *cobwebs* over that window." The window was too small to allow anyone to come through without breaking the cobwebs. Dust on the sill was undisturbed. And the scuff mark could easily have been left when John entered earlier, in the summer.

Steve told me that the FBI left before the child was even found. They knew it wasn't a kidnapping. They knew immediately. And you know how they knew? Because they have done this before. They have experience.

Steve told me that he asked Patsy if she fed JonBenét anything before she put her to bed and Patsy said no, absolutely not. But the coroner found undigested pineapple bits in the upper part of her large intestine. Then they found a bowl of pineapple bits with Patsy's fingerprints on it. The JonBenét websites are so detailed they have special links to each piece of evidence, including one reserved entirely for "the pineapple evidence." They have scoured the earth to find experts who will argue that digestion itself can be extended by many hours under certain conditions—that maybe JonBenét ate the pineapple *before* the Ramseys went to the Christmas party that night. Nonsense.

Talk about grasping desperately at straws. Patsy Ramsey did not want to admit she gave JonBenét that pineapple because there was something connected to that, which she wanted to avoid. What was it?

Why lie about something so innocuous? In my experience, there is always a reason. It means JonBenét was awake in the house that night, and did not, as the Ramseys insisted, sleep solidly as her father carried her from the car to her bedroom.

You can see from the outset what plagued the situation: these people were so affluent, so "normal," so powerful and well-known in Boulder, that it took a very long time for suspicion to mount against them at all. The whole scene—from the outset—was treated as one in which John and Patsy Ramsey had to be made as *comfortable* as possible.

Over the next ten days, investigators collected evidence in a climate that had begun to turn strangely uphill. They had to struggle from the outset to make sure it was *okay* with the Ramseys that they did their jobs.

When Steve Thomas went into the case, the mandate he was given was, "Unscrew this."

Yet, Thomas was not able to interview the Ramseys for two full months after the murders. Immediately after JonBenét's death, Patsy was placed on heavy sedation, and investigators were told by John that she was in "no condition" to submit to a police interview.

Soon the various players were drawn into a cat's cradle of "negotiations" about the conditions of the interview, and the terms were dictated, absurdly, by the Ramseys and their attorneys, with the five primary detectives, including Thomas, hamstrung.

They claimed they didn't submit to polygraphs because they had been advised not to. John Ramsey, in the interview that finally transpired with Steve Thomas, said: "Well, what I've been told is that, and I felt tremendous guilt after we lost JonBenét, because I hadn't protected her, like I failed as a parent. And was told that that's, with that kind of emotion, you shouldn't take a lie detector test because you did have that guilt feeling."

Polygraphs work by measuring the consistency of bodily functions. When someone with no mental defect, who is well-rested, and not under the influence of drugs or alcohol tells a lie, their body responds in certain consistent ways. So feeling guilty has nothing to do with what your body reveals—telling the truth, or hiding in lies.

The Ramseys later hired their own experts to do polygraph tests and it was announced that they passed. However, polygraph tests administered by experts for defense attorneys are meaningless to an investigating detective. He can't watch the test, he has no access to the tapes of a suspect's reactions to particular questions so can't do any follow-up, and he has no control over what the suspect was asked (preventing him from using any inside information he has or gathering information the suspect doesn't consider damaging). He can't put the suspect in a controlled situation in order to gain the information he needs to either move forward towards charges or exonerate him. And of course, no defense attorney is ever going to announce *how many* polygraph tests it might take to get his client to pass—or what carefully worded questions allowed the client to speak around or evade the truth.

The main reason I believe to this day that the murderer was somebody who lived in that house—and I believe it was Patsy—is that there is absolutely no evidence to the contrary. There are no signs of a break-in. Virtually no foreign DNA or fingerprints or eyewitness accounts. Nobody heard anything. The cobwebs on the window in the basement were undisturbed, so nobody entered there. Every expert who looked at the case, including the FBI, said it looked like the scene had been staged. The cause of death was asphyxiation, and she had an 8.5-inch vertical skull fracture that caused bruising on the brain, but produced so little blood it was thought to have occurred when she was dead or dying. She had been bound with ligature around her neck and wrists, and blood and abrasions were found in her vaginal area. No semen was evident. It was inconclusive whether she had been sexually assaulted during the attack that killed her—but she showed *chronic* inflammation of the vaginal wall and had only half her hymen. Outspoken forensic pathologist Dr. Cyril Wecht, who reviewed the autopsy photos and evidence, noted that he had been informed that the police had called in three separate child abuse experts, and that they had concluded, separately and independently, that "there was evidence of prior sexual abuse."

People tend to want to deny the possibility that a child has been sexually abused. Wecht stepped forward and said what others refused to say. Whereas media reports focused intently on the fact that there was not clear evidence of sexual assault when JonBenét was killed, there was another elephant in the room that became invisible. Wecht stated point blank:

> It's the most ridiculous thing in the world, a little girl with half of her hymen gone and she's dead, and you've got a tiny abrasion, a tiny contusion, and a chronic inflammation of the vaginal mucosa. That means it happened more than 72 hours earlier; we don't know how long, or how often it was repeated, but chronic means it wasn't from that night. This was a tragic, tragic accident. This was a game that had been played before.

There was other evidence of JonBenét being a chronically molested child. Bedwetting is a "telltale" sign of sexual abuse. JonBenét was a bedwetter, and had urinated in her pajamas the night she died. Patsy kept a rubber sheet on her bed and used Pull-Up diapers on her, a box of which were opened as if recently accessed in JonBenét's bathroom. In Patsy Ramsey's interview with officers Steve Thomas and Tom Trujillo, she addressed the bedwetting blithely and inadvertently revealed more bombshells:

> **TT:** The 25th, during the day of the 25th, do you recall seeing any injuries on JonBenét? Any scratches, abrasions, cuts, bruises, or anything like that?
>
> **PR:** I don't remember, but she was always getting bruised, you know. Kids just, I don't remember anything. . . . She would tend to have more respiratory kind of stuff.
>
> **TT:** And just on this, just a little bit, JonBenét wet the bed every once and awhile?
>
> **PR:** Yeah.
>
> **TT:** About how often would that occur?
>
> **PR:** Oh, maybe once a week or something.
>
> **TT:** Ok.
>
> **PR:** If I just didn't take her to the potty and make her go to the potty before bedtime, she very likely would wet the bed.
>
> **TT:** OK. You have any idea about, has this been going on for how long? Any time that she broken [sic] and didn't have any bed wetting problems and then started back up or anything like that.

PR: No, no, she just, I mean I've had her in Pull-Ups until very recently. I kind of thought it might be better, I mean Pull-Ups and those Pamper things are so absorbent, that you can't you know, the child can't feel if they're wet or not. So I thought well it might just be better if she felt wet than being...

TT: (Inaudible)

PR: Yeah. But she had a lot of dry nights, but she would wet the bed probably once a week.

TT: When she wet the bed, would she come up and tell you guys, or would she just crawl onto the other bed, crawl into Burke's spare bed, what was the routine if she actually wet the bed?

PR: Well, ah, sometimes she would get up and get into the other bed or sometimes she really wouldn't wake up and until morning when she normally would wake up and maybe she'd change her nightgown or something and I'd find her things and pajamas in the bathroom floors and...

TT: OK. Is this something you guys (inaudible) about at all?

PR: No, cause I mean, all of, Burke wore Pull-Ups, you know till he was, at night, you know. Till he was fairly old. And Melinda was, we didn't even have Pull-Ups back then, she wet the bed till she was, I mean at least when we were married, she was 8 then. So I didn't see anything, and a lot of our friends, I mean, and Matthew used to wear Pull-Ups, you know, so...

TT: So, it wasn't anything out of the ordinary.

PR: Uh-huh, no.

TT: OK. How did John feel about this, did he have any reason to...

PR: I don't know if he even knew.

TT: OK. This was something that you took care of?

PR: Uh-huh.

TT: OK. When JonBenét would wet the bed weekly, who took care of the sheets? Is that something Linda had to take care of? How often, I guess, who would even clean the sheets, to be more specific.

PR: Well, she normally changed the beds weekly, but typically, it the, as seen as, you know I, Linda didn't come in till 9 o'clock. But typically, I would strip the bed, you know, put them in the washer or something.

TT: OK.

PR: Before she got there.

TT: Do you remember back in '94, typical doctor's visit, you fill out all those forms, making some sort of a notation, on one of Dr. Beuf's forms about bed-wetting and soiling. That was kind of a concern, you remember anything?

PR: No, before was when I was having chemotherapy. I don't remember. Susanne took them to the doctor a lot then. My housekeeper, a nanny sort of. I don't remember. I mean if...

TT: Do you recall filling out these so-called, yes/no question type forms back then?

PR: If I saw it I might remember it.

TT: OK. Anyone that you can recall that would show any inappropriate affection towards JonBenét? Anybody out in the pageant circuit, friends, neighbors, anybody like that?
PR: No.

Here we learn that JonBenét, as well as her brother Burke, as well as John Ramsey's daughter from his previous marriage, were all bed-wetters many years past the normal toilet training stage. And you can see from Patsy's comments that she has arranged to be 100 percent unperturbed and clueless about this, rationalizing it as perfectly normal and prattling on about Pull-Ups,® as if that were the issue.

TT: Right. And one of those had something about a kitty game, that was her favorite game. You remember what that's about?
PR: Kitty?
TT: Yeah.
PR: To play kitty. Yeah, she likes to play kitty (inaudible).
TT: Uh.
PR: You don't like kitty, huh. She and Daphne like to, they love kittens. And we had some kittens up at the lake (inaudible). And she and Daphne like to pretend they were kittens. She's just, they would walk around and they would say, oh there's a kitty, (inaudible). Let's go into the pet shop, I think I'll buy this one.
TT: And that's the game JonBenét really liked or something?

> **PR:** She and Daphne played kitty. They'd walk around
> on all fours, you know.
> **TT:** Ah, you have anything else, Steve.
> **ST:** You guys need a short break, or do you want to keep
> going?

What on earth does Patsy mean when she says to Detective Trujillo, "You don't like kitty, huh?"

As if it's a game he must be perfectly familiar with. As if it's something real to her, as real as it would be to a young child.

Something was very wrong in this family. It's just *there*.

But leaving *all of that* disturbing strangeness aside as well, let's talk about the main thing:

The central piece of evidence was the ransom note—2 $\frac{1}{2}$ pages long, written on a pad from her kitchen using a pen still there, in a cup. Out of thirty-seven suspects, Patsy Ramsey was the only one whose handwriting sample could not rule her out. That, to me, is devastating. Here is how Patsy addresses it, in an exchange with Steve Thomas:

> **ST:** If it's appropriate, Patsy, and you're not involved and
> you know we're still trying to determine whether you're
> in the bucket or out of the bucket, I hope that if you
> ever get out of that bucket.
> **PR:** What's the in the bucket, out of the bucket mean?
> **ST:** Well, let me give you that analogy. There is a num-
> ber of people, a list if you will, that we certainly have to
> include or exclude off that list. I can only appreciate
> what your life's been like for the last four months, but

what we're working towards is the resolution that we'll reach in this thing. If this is somebody you knew, Patsy, if this offender was somebody that you knew, who would have had the best opportunity to have committed this crime by entering your home, writing the note inside your home, and I don't think it's a far reach to say that the note was written inside the house given the circumstance with the pad and the character comparison and so forth.

PR: I don't know what the, ah ...

ST: The note was written from a pad inside the home.

PR: It was?

ST: Uh-huh.

PR: Oh, I didn't know that.

She didn't *know* that? What planet had she been on? That detail would have been established in the first hours of her daughter's disappearance.

In another exchange, Thomas presses her further:

"We're seeing some indications that you may have authored that note. Is there any reason you can think of, why these experts would say that?"

Patsy replied:

I, I mean, I don't, I'm not a handwriting person. I've given handwriting after handwriting after handwriting. You know, maybe it's a female that wrote the note. I mean, I don't know. I mean, I don't know how to analyze handwriting, but I'm sure they're doing the best that they know how to do. But, I don't know what else to do, you know. I write like I write.

In her answer, she talks too much. If asked this question, an innocent person would be short and simple. "No! I didn't write the note. How could you say that?"

Patsy described being on numerous drugs—sedatives and anti-depressants—which her husband took as well. In fact, so did just about every person involved in this case, when asked, in deposition, "Are you on any medication?" They almost all—including Arndt—listed anti-depressants and/or sedatives.

Why was she in a perpetual fog? What was she trying to forget or escape from, not be conscious of?

She claimed not even to have any earthly idea whether she ever got the basement window fixed yet recalled sweeping up all the glass. Look at her language here:

> **TT:** When did John break that window in the basement?
>
> **PR:** He, I don't know exactly when he did it, but I think it was last summer sometime when we, the kids and I were at the lake.
>
> **TT:** In Charlevoix.
>
> **PR:** In Charlevoix and he told me to come back from out of town or whatever and he didn't have a key and the only way he could get in was to break the window.
>
> **TT:** Okay.
>
> **PR:** The little um, like door, little window to the basement there.

TT: He had to lift the grate out of the way too, to get in there.

PR: Yeah, that's the one, um hum.

TT: Okay. Any reason why that one wasn't replaced or the pane wasn't fixed or anything?

PR: No, I don't know whether I fixed it or didn't fix it. I can't remember even trying to remember that, um, I remember when I got back, uh, in the fall, you know . . .

TT: Um hum.

PR: . . . Uh, went down there and cleaned up all the glass.

TT: Okay.

PR: I mean I cleaned that thoroughly and I asked Linda to go behind me and vacuum. I mean I picked up every chunk, I mean, because the kids played down there in that back area back there.

TT: Um hum.

PR: And I mean I scoured that place when, cause they were always down there. Burke particularly and the boys would go down there and play with cars and things and uh, there was just a ton of glass everywhere.

TT: Okay.

PR: And I cleaned all that up and then she, she vacuumed a couple of times down there.

TT: To get all the glass.

PR: In the fall, yeah, cause it was just little, you know, pieces, big pieces, everything.

TT: Do you ever recall getting that window replaced?

PR: Yeah, uh, I can't remember. I just can't remember whether I got it replaced or not.

If you had to go through the hassle of getting a basement window replaced, you'd remember it. She's lying. She's often lying. But why?

Again, the window is something that in her mind leads down a path she doesn't want to go down. It seems trivial, yet she's lying about it. People lie for a reason.

In conclusion, let's imagine what the killer would have been thinking to him or herself in order for the intruder theory to hold water:

> I know what I'll do, I'll break into the Ramsey home on Christmas night. The alarm system is probably not on. I'll go get JonBenét, take her to the basement, have my way with her. They won't wake up. No way they will be up at 11:00 p.m. on Christmas night. What a perfect night for me to commit this crime. Oh wait! I forgot to bring paper and pen to write the ransom note. Oh good, in the kitchen there are samples of Patsy's handwriting. I'll make it look *kinda* like her handwriting. I'll do a draft to practice so I get the note right and leave it in the house. I'll make it look like a kidnapping, but I won't call to collect the money, even though they obviously would get it for me right away to save their daughter. I won't leave any traces of myself, and even when I carry the child down that creaking staircase, I am certain they won't wake up. People sleep really deeply on Christmas night. It's a perfect plan. I know I'll get away with it.

Yeah. Right. Even if it was a botched kidnapping as intruder theorists speculate, why wouldn't the aspiring kidnapper take her body with him to secure the ransom from her parents with no way of knowing she wasn't alive? The answer is clear: she was left because this wasn't a kidnapping.

Patsey Ramsey died of ovarian cancer in 2006, taking many answers to questions crucial for solving the case with her to the grave.

In 2008, Boulder District Attorney Mary Lacy announced to the press that the Ramseys had been fully exonerated by three pieces of foreign male DNA found on JonBenét's long johns and panties, acquired by scraping the sides of the cloth for skin cells, so called "touch DNA."

On July 9, 2008, Cyril Wecht addressed the new findings. "The fact that this other DNA was found at this time matches previous DNA that was thought to be a contaminant does not then alter the picture." Of course not. This did not call for the public exoneration the DA rushed to give; it called for investigation. There was no way to know whether it belonged to the killer—her body as well as the crime scene was hopelessly contaminated from the start. And the killer still walks free. And District Attorney Lacy gets to grandstand, and write an apology letter to the family. And the press ate it up, learning nothing from the ways they compromised the investigation with their false leads, leaked information, and overexposure.

Some things never change. JonBenét still lies in her grave, dressed in her best pageant gown, a sparkling tiara on her head, waiting for justice.

CHAPTER SEVEN

THE STRANGE DEATH OF A WHITE HOUSE COUNSEL: VINCE FOSTER

HERE'S A TIP THAT MAY SOUND CALLOUS. If you plan to commit suicide, do your loved ones a favor and make it *abundantly* clear. Choose perhaps a bridge during rush hour.

You may not want to blow your brains out on live television, like disgraced politician Bud Dwyer did, but you really should, out of respect, make sure you have reliable witnesses of some kind.

But whatever you do, don't go into a vast park you have no connection to, with a gun not familiar to your wife, with bullets not traceable to your stash, leaving no definitive note, telling no one, promising your secretary you'll be back shortly, and hope that everybody is able to work it all out after you're gone. Don't be in that much of a hurry. Please. Write a suicide note that actually has your fingerprints on it, at *least*. And don't tear it into thirty-seven pieces and put it in your briefcase. Especially if you are the Deputy Counsel to a scandal-plagued, power-mad administration.

On July 20, 1993, Deputy White House counsel and attorney to Bill and Hillary Clinton, Vince Foster, was found dead in Fort Marcy State Park, seven miles from the White House, from a gunshot wound to the head. That much we all agree on. We also all agree that for some unfathomable reason, the White House was satisfied with the Park Police leading the investigation into Foster's death. Foster's body was found in front of the barrel of one of two cannons remaining from an old Civil War fort. There was no blood or brain matter on the surrounding foliage. His right hand was still on the trigger of the .38 caliber handgun, and his body was lying very neatly.

If Foster's death had been determined a homicide, he would have been the highest-ranking government official killed since JFK.

But immediately, when the news broke, Park Police reports assured the American public that it was a suicide. It wasn't really considered or investigated as a possible homicide—it was so *clearly* a suicide. Maybe the FBI failed to take over the scene because they were dealing with then President Clinton firing their beleaguered director, William Sessions, the day before. Why *not* let the Park Police handle the death scene of one of the most powerful men in the White House? They did well. They only moved his head a few times, they saw nothing suspicious at the scene, and since they saw a gun in his hand, expertly concluded that it was a suicide.

I don't know if anybody ever taught the Park Police standard police protocol, which requires any violent death to be treated first as a homicide, unless and until it can be definitively ruled otherwise. But the White House was not concerned, so why should they be? Foster's death was called a suicide in the amount of time it takes to say

Another Investigation Hopelessly Corrupted by Power. This time, guess who dictated the investigation, interfered with critical evidence, rushed the autopsy, and made sure few, if any, proper crime and forensics procedures were followed, starting with a full homicide investigation and questioning of everybody the man crossed paths with? The White House. They didn't even know where Foster had been all afternoon. And they didn't seem to care.

No sooner had Foster been found dead than White House staff started carting boxes of files from his office and attempting to gain access to his safe. I know it sounds like a bad movie. It sounds like *All the President's Men*. If you want to know *all* the details of this, you'll have to descend to the bowels of the Internet, where "conspiracies" flourish unchecked.

But we all know: to care or read or pay attention to this is to go down a rabbit hole that has been reserved strictly for tin-foil hat, right-wing "loons." It's as easy as that. We say "tin-foil hat, right-wing loons," and we're done. We don't have to think about Vince Foster anymore.

But I'm still a cop. I don't quite get why it is that you have to be a "staunch" conservative, or any other kind of conservative, to think that, for example, a bullet through the mouth produces a gushing splatter of blood and brains. Or that a "suicide note" declared by three experts not just a forgery, but an "obvious" forgery, isn't exactly proof of suicide.

Foster, the world was told via the media, was "depressed" and "under a lot of pressure."

Oh and he was *so* upset at the *Wall Street Journal*, whose editors "lie without consequence," and are so mean to the Clinton Administration. Suddenly, Foster had been "wrestling" with depression. (He had been prescribed an anti-depressant called Trazodone the day before.) But why would he commit suicide like this? No warning—nothing. In a park, in the middle of the day, with family vacation plans imminent, and without a word of goodbye or a goodbye letter that was *not* about how misunderstood the Clintons are. That would have been a good start—to make the official story credible.

Foster left his office in the White House at 1:00 p.m. that day, after eating a burger and fries at his desk. In parting, he told his secretary Linda Tripp that there were M&Ms on the tray if she wanted some. With his jacket slung over his shoulder and no briefcase, he walked out, saying to Tripp, "I'll be back."

He never returned.

Around 4:30 p.m., a motorist named Patrick Knowlton, whose life has been forever changed by this moment, needed urgently to take a leak. Knowlton chose a most remarkable time and place in history to do so. It was about seventy minutes before Foster's body was found, by yet another motorist who needed to urinate and actually wound up near the body by a fluke. That person is known only as "CW" in the Fiske report, which stands for "confidential witness," whereas Knowlton is known as "C2" in Ken Starr's report. Patrick Knowlton didn't see the body, but he saw something else extremely significant, at least to a non-corrupt member of law enforcement.

Knowlton later filed a civil lawsuit against a Park Police sergeant, the Deputy Chief Medical examiner, a pathologist, six FBI agents, and seven "John Doe" harassers, who, among them, intimidated, assaulted, and followed him. They accused him publicly of being mentally ill and a homosexual, orchestrated severe intimidation and harassment against him, and forged his testimony in a report that went to the Grand Jury. In his lawsuit, he told his story as follows:

On July 20, 1993, between the time of 3:00 p.m. and 4:00 p.m., Vincent Foster died of a small-caliber gunshot wound to his head, at the hand of another. The bullet entered his head from the upper portion of the right side of his neck, under the jaw line, passed upward through the body of the tongue, pierced his brain and struck the skull approximately three inches below the top of the head, fracturing it. The bullet remained in his head. Blood drained from the entrance wound in the neck onto his right collar and shoulder and was absorbed down onto his right shirtsleeve. Blood also accumulated in his mouth.

Also on July 20, 1993, Plaintiff was driving on the George Washington Memorial Parkway. In heavy traffic and facing over a two-hour commute, Plaintiff pulled into Fort Marcy Park at 4:30 p.m. to relieve himself. Plaintiff parked close to the main footpath entrance into the park, between the only two cars in the small parking lot, which were parked just four spaces apart.

To Plaintiff's left was parked an unoccupied mid-1980s rust-brown four-door Honda sedan with Arkansas tags (closest to the footpath entrance), and on his right was a late model metallic blue-gray sedan, backed into its parking space. A man was seated in the driver's seat of the blue-gray sedan. Immediately after Plaintiff parked, the man lowered the passenger side electric window and stared at him, menacingly, which unnerved Plaintiff as he exited his car.

As he started from his car toward the footpath, Plaintiff heard the blue-gray sedan's door open. Apprehensive, Plaintiff walked to the sign bordering the footpath entrance to the park and feigned to read its historical information while nonchalantly glancing to his right to see if the man was approaching. He saw the man leaning on the roof of the driver's side of his blue-gray sedan, watching him intently. Plaintiff then cautiously proceeded seventy-five feet down the footpath's left fork to the first large tree, in the opposite direction from which Mr. Foster's body was later recovered.

As he relieved himself, Plaintiff heard the man close his car door. Because the foliage was dense, he could not see whether the man was approaching. As Plaintiff walked back to the parking lot with a heightened sense of awareness, he scanned the lot but did not see the man. Plaintiff surmised that the man had either gotten back in his car or perhaps could even be crouching between the brown Honda and Plaintiff's car.

In order to maintain his distance from the space between the Honda and his own car until he learned the man's whereabouts, Plaintiff walked directly toward the driver's side door of the Honda, and then around the back of it. As Plaintiff reached the driver's side door of the brown Honda, he looked through the window. He also looked into the back seat as he walked the length of that car. He saw a dark-colored suit jacket draped over the driver's seat, a briefcase on the front passenger's seat, and two bottles of wine cooler on the back seat. As he reached the back of the Honda, Plaintiff was relieved to see that the man had returned to his own vehicle. The man was still staring fixedly at him.

Patrick Knowlton is a fascinating figure in the saga of Vince Foster, because he is the only "real" person involved—not enmeshed in any of the three pre-determined investigations, not answerable to the White House, FBI, or any other central power—he was just a guy, relieving himself. His life was all but destroyed by what he witnessed.

What does this tell us about Vince Foster's death, and the society we live in, and particularly the media, who never once told you about Patrick Knowlton—only about those *hopelessly paranoid conservatives* and their "lurid imaginations" (*Newsweek*) regarding the Foster affair. Not only did they vehemently, proudly *ignore* the Gorilla-in-the-Room Foster story, they went out of their way to create a new story in its place, that was, naturally, all about the fools, nuts, whack jobs, and seething "right wingers" who *just won't let the story die,* and can't "accept" the "conclusion" of "three investigations" that Vince Foster "committed suicide."

Let's look at it another way. Why were three investigations necessary if this was such a straightforward suicide? Why were witnesses harassed, even assaulted, and why did the FBI alter testimonies? Just to speed up the "obvious" conclusion?

There are excellent and brave journalistic accounts of this mess, most notably Chris Ruddy's *The Strange Death of Vincent Foster*.

Patrick Knowlton and his courageous attorney John Clarke documented their case carefully in a book you've never heard of called *Failure of the Public Trust,* published in 1999. The "real" journalists meanwhile, like *60 Minutes'* Mike Wallace, are paid millions of dollars a year not to tell us what *happened,* but to tell us why we mustn't trust people who say something very bad might have happened. This elite class devoted themselves to the eye-rolling story of how unfounded and crazy the "conspiracy" theories were and how tiring they found it to "deal" with them—never mind how much it must have exhausted the poor Clintons.

Maybe it's all my years as a cop that cured me of the delusion so many seem to suffer from that oh no, people don't do bad things. But as that English lord pointed out, "Power corrupts."

The reason this story won't die is that the *investigation* was almost mind-bogglingly unorthodox, to put it mildly.

One of the most powerful men in the White House was found dead in a public park, with a gunshot wound, and the *Park Police* were left in charge of investigating the crime scene. American citizens who die in plane crashes in foreign countries get investigations by the FBI, but a White House Deputy Counsel dead from a gunshot wound within a stone's throw of the White House is investigated by the Park Police? Are you kidding me?

And they wonder why 60 percent of the American people have misgivings about the story that Vince Foster committed suicide.

The Park Police are not equipped to handle *any* death investigation, let alone somebody from the White House. They are not forensically equipped, they don't have the right training, and they are not experienced. Every forensic investigative body that is centralized in the country—FBI, FBI labs, CIA, Secret Service—is within a moment's drive from this crime scene. Why did the FBI not handle the scene?

I also know a thing or two about people blowing their brains out. And in this case, the scene does not fit the manner of death at all.

If you shoot yourself in the mouth with a gun of any kind, there is going to be an extreme amount of blood leaving the sinus area. No two ways about it. Go on YouTube, if you're not squeamish, and look at the footage of Budd Dwyer who put a .357 magnum revolver in his mouth and pulled the trigger. The amount of blood that poured from his head was like two garden hoses turned on full blast. His head was not unique in this regard.

Yet Vince Foster, we are led to believe, put a gun in his mouth, pulled the trigger, and left almost no blood, and no mess at all in the foliage around him.

Why was there no blood or brain tissue in the surrounding area? There should have been "high velocity" blood and tissue splatter in the surrounding area. Yet there wasn't, and Foster was found with very little blood on him, and a clotted, matted wound at the back of his head.

Why were carpet fibers on his clothes? Are any of them in his car, discovered at the scene? Presuming that he drove the car there, we should find similar carpet fibers on the seat or vehicle's carpet on the driver's side of his car. If those fibers were present in another location in the car, then we can assume that is where he was located on the way to Fort Marcy Park. If there were no carpet fibers anywhere in the car, because of the numerous fibers on his body, we would have to conclude Vince Foster was not in his car between the time those fibers were acquired and he was found dead.

Why did he take his reading glasses and not his sunglasses into the park on a sunny day? Why was there no soil on his shoes? Why was the area leading up to the body trampled as if several people had walked there? Why were his glasses seventeen feet from his body?

Why didn't the forensics match the scene? If Vince Foster did commit suicide, did he commit suicide in Fort Marcy Park?

The questions that were never answered raise very legitimate concerns, and cast doubt on the official version of the story. And I say that as a detective, with vast experience in both homicide and suicide investigations. Questions must be answered, and can be answered, but first they have to be *asked*. When you have politics and death, it appears that the media walks very gingerly. I don't know why.

Based on the information the public has been given, I would say he did not commit suicide in Fort Marcy Park. That being so, it means that even if he committed suicide somewhere else and was moved, it *becomes* a murder investigation. If you move somebody who had committed suicide, it is virtually impossible to prove that it is not a murder.

A lot of excellent investigative work has been done on this case—it just wasn't done by the U.S. government or members of the mainstream media. As Chris Ruddy reported in his 1997 book, *The Strange Death of Vincent Foster*, two New York City Police homicide detectives—Vincent Scalice and Fred Santucci—were hired by the conservative-backed Western Journalism Center in 1994 to reconstruct the crime scene and review all of the forensic evidence. They concluded after a four-month investigation that the "overwhelming evidence" was that Foster's body was moved to the park. Scalice had twenty years of experience with crime scenes and forensics, and Santucci had logged fifteen years as a forensic crime scene photographer and twenty-seven years as a cop. Scalice and Santucci reported, among other things, that:

- The gun had none of Foster's fingerprints on it, though conditions were ideal for them.
- The gun could not be identified by Foster's family as being his. It was an antique gun made from parts of two more weapons, with two serial numbers traceable to 1913.
- It had only two bullets in its cylinder. No matching ammunition was found in the Foster homes. (Would Foster, a gun owner, go to such lengths not to use one of his own guns?)
- No one heard the gunshot, in a park with people in close proximity and excellent acoustics.
- There was a small amount of blood at the scene. There was no blood, brain tissue, or bone in the surrounding vegetation. (The area should have been sprayed with these materials in the explosion created by the blast.)
- Twenty officials on the scene that night confirmed that the surrounding area showed no blood splatter.
- Foster's shoes were found by an FBI lab not to have a speck of soil on them, despite his supposedly walking through 800 feet of grass and brush, to arrive at the spot where he is said to have shot himself.

- When the detectives had two men of Foster's build walk the same path, "significant" amounts of soil were found on their shoes.
- FBI labs found "blond to light brown" head hairs, that were not Foster's, and six different colors of carpet fibers, on every article of his clothing, including his underwear.
- The first person to discover Foster's body, CW, saw trampled vegetation leading to his body. Park Police said there was no disturbed vegetation.

But these findings have not been investigated by the media—even though they've known about them. On the tenth anniversary of Foster's death, Patrick Knowlton produced an audio-presentation by U.S. Attorney Miquel Rodriguez who had been hired by Kenneth Starr to conduct a Grand Jury investigation into Foster's death, only to resign when he found that the conclusions were pre-ordained.

Knowlton said, in his introduction:

> Since July 20, 1993, when the body of deputy White House counsel Vincent Foster was found at Fort Marcy Park, the American government, and more importantly, the American press, have concealed the true facts of the death from the American people.
>
> Now, ten years later, we hear from the leading government investigator that Foster did not die the way officials have said. We now learn firsthand—from the person in charge of Independent Counsel Kenneth Starr's Foster death investigation—that Starr's investi-

gation was a sham and that its conclusion was determined even before the investigation even began. Investigators altered the crime scene, and a few people controlled the outcome of the investigation. The press controlled how it would be reported.

You are about to hear the voice of Miquel Rodriguez, a United States Attorney working in Sacramento, California.

Mr. Rodriguez resigned from Kenneth Starr's office of Independent Counsel in the spring of 1995, when Kenneth Starr's staff frustrated his investigation. Mr. Rodriguez resigned because he refused to participate in covering up Foster's murder. Mr. Rodriguez revealed the truth to over a hundred people—journalists, congressmen, senators, and others, in his attempts to get the facts of the case to the public. What you will hear are actual excerpts from some of these conversations....

Rodriguez said he presented his fully documented case to over 100 journalists, to no avail:

I have talked to a number of people that—you know, from *Time* magazine, *Newsweek*, *Nightline*, the *New York Times*, *Boston Globe*, the *Atlanta* [Journal Constitution]... there have been well over a hundred, and it risks—this matter is so sealed tight... the reporters are all genuinely interested but... when they start to get excited and they've got a story and they're ready to go, the editors.... They went to all the trouble of writing, and then it got killed.... I know the *New York Times* has it—knows, and just won't... I know that they won't do anything about it and I do know that, that many people have called me back. Reporters that I've spent a lot of time with called me back and said the editors won't allow it to go to press. The accepted media here has always had... a certain take on all of this. And there's been storylines from the get-go.

Despite these suspicious circumstances, the mass media reserve the right to totally ignore a huge story that involves government malfeasance. Anyone interested in investigating the story they've chosen to ignore runs the risk of being accused of formulating "conspiracy theories," which is just about the lowest thing you can do in media-land, where nothing too strange ever happens, and everybody merrily eats steamed clams together on Martha's Vineyard. These people are the elite, and the elite are not the worrying class. Worrying about things, sounding alarms, digging, investigating—all of that causes a downward trajectory in a journalist's career—unless of course you're digging in a sandbox that has been designated by the "respectable" media as scandal terrain. By and large though, investigations give them all dyspepsia, and "conspiracy" is the best dismissive word anybody ever gave them; it's as bad as "mental illness." "Theories" sounds like the direct opposite of evidence, so it's perfect for the superiority complex of most lazy, cowardly journalists. Another good word is "fringe," which speaks for itself.

As you may know, I was actually crazy enough to tackle the JFK assassination to see if I could find something new. In my book, *A Simple Act of Murder,* I concluded that JFK was killed by a lone gunman and that gunman was Oswald. It was simple. But once the waters got muddied, it seemed infinitely complex. It really wasn't.

Any honest person can see that however and wherever Vince Foster died, he did not die in Fort Marcy Park. What did die in Fort Marcy Park was any sliver of hope any of us may still have had that we have anything resembling a free press in this country willing to investigate, report, or stand up to a difficult set of facts.

We have come full circle from where this book began. I told you that murder is of great interest to the media, and we looked at cases of pretty women and cute toddlers who were murdered, and the rapacious, infinite, and detailed interest the media took in those cases. *Newsweek's* word—"lurid"—is more fitting here than it is when aimed at those who would like to see the Foster case taken up in the mass media. Those cases were perhaps gripping, but they were not important. Yet no expense was spared searching for every imaginable witness or calling on countless experts to analyze forensic evidence. The whole culture, from the cop shows to the Murder Media, is awash in "whodunnit" obsession. But not when it comes to one of the most powerful men (at the time) in the White House. Suddenly, they've all lost interest in forensics and ballistics and blood pools and all the rest. They won't take the story even when it is served to them on a platter with the most gleaming, impeccable sources imaginable. Actually, let me correct that. Some of them would take the story, if they were allowed to run it. But the majority of the media is like a protective nanny. Despite 60 percent of the American people thinking something is amiss in Vince Foster's death, they refuse to cover it. They shut their collective eyes to avoid accounting for evidence and details that one in two Americans reasonably doubts.

In 1997, my then-writing partner Stephen Weeks and I went to Fort Marcy Park and examined the scene (this was before the area was re-landscaped by the White House). We wrote a book proposal about Vince Foster's death, which we brought to every major publishing house. None of them would touch it with a ten-foot pole. We weren't saying how he died—to this day I have no idea. Nor am I willing to speculate. All I know for sure—because I know crime scenes—is where Foster did *not* die. He did not die in Fort Marcy Park.

CHAPTER EIGHT

THE CASE THAT STARTED IT ALL: O. J. SIMPSON

BEFORE NATALIE HOLLOWAY DISAPPEARED in Aruba, before Nancy Grace started up her drumbeat commentary on crime, before Fox News Channel even existed, there was one murder case that single-handedly launched the modern era of true crime TV news, one case that forever placed the pursuit of justice second-fiddle to the pursuit of 24/7 coverage and blockbuster Nielson ratings. It was the most widely covered case in the history of mass media. I know, because I was at ground-zero. That case, of course, was the investigation, arrest, and trial of O. J. Simpson.

I played, as you may know, a pivotal role in that case. I have written a best-selling book about it. I have been interviewed about it countless times. And yet, I have never before told the story start to finish, as it actually was. I knew I would tell the full story some day, when the hysteria had died down, when the media was no longer beating down on it, distorting it, and spinning it—and when enough time passed for there to be no risk of more innocent people suffering the career destruction I've seen firsthand.

One such innocent person was my former partner, Brad Roberts, who probably did more than any other detective in finding evidence that should have convicted O. J. Simpson. Despite his crucial role, he was kept out of the trial and ignored by the media. The evidence he found was misconstrued and misrepresented—and he was unable to stop it from happening. Much of what follows is his untold story, as it happened and as we both remember. In fact, in preparation for this book, I went over these chapters with him to make sure nothing was left out. He stood behind the facts you are about to read.

As you will see though, this case attracted record-breaking media coverage, yet every investigative reporter, every news editor, every nightly news broadcaster missed the real story. The demands of our 24-hour-a-day reality TV—demands for instant news in ever-shorter soundbites, and ever higher ratings—distracted the media from doing their job. Though I was falsely accused of perjury, they missed uncovering what some would call acts of perjury and obstruction of justice. And in the end, a cold-blooded killer got away with murder.

It all began with a phone call in the early morning of June 13, 1994, back when I was a homicide detective in the West LA Division of the LAPD. It was 1:05 a.m. and I had been asleep for a couple hours. I had no doubt it was the office calling. Since I wasn't on call that night, I could have just let the phone ring. But when you're a cop and the phone rings in the middle of the night, it usually means there has been a homicide, and that people are waiting for you to arrive and turn chaos into some kind of order. It's a good feeling when somebody needs you, and it's your job to help them.

So I picked up the phone.

My boss, Ron Phillips, told me that two bodies had been found in front of 845 South Bundy Drive, the residence of Nicole Brown, O. J. Simpson's ex-wife. One victim was a Caucasian female, possibly Brown herself. The other victim was a Caucasian male, also unidentified at the time, who turned out to be Ron Goldman.

Phillips asked me to help on the case. Though my partner Brad Roberts was on call that night and would be coming in, too, I was the only other homicide detective in the area and Brad would need help. So I told Phillips I'd meet him at West LA station.

Phillips and I drove to Bundy together, arriving at 2:10 a.m. Patrol officer Robert Riske showed us the crime scene. There were bloodstains all over the cobblestone walkway and canine paw prints in blood leading away from the house. Inside the front gate, we saw the female victim: a white woman in a short black dress. Maybe she had been pretty; it was hard to tell. She was face down in a pool of blood, her hair so saturated that we didn't know whether she was a blonde or brunette.

The male victim was lying face up in the bushes on the other side of the walkway. We could see a leather glove and a black knit stocking cap nearby. There was a wet shine to the area close to the victim, which was probably his own blood soaked into the ground.

Riske led us through the house and out the back door. When he was finished showing us what he had observed, Riske took Phillips down the alley and around to the front of the house by the street. I went back through the crime scene, writing down various observations and possible items of evidence.

One of my first thoughts was that the victims didn't match. The female victim was dressed for indoors with a short dress and bare feet. The male victim was dressed for outdoors with a jacket and shoes. Inside the house, candles were lit and the bath was filled with water. She could have been waiting for someone. Maybe she answered the door. It might have been a love triangle or an attempted residential robbery.

We didn't know the cause of death yet, but a trail of blood drops led to the back alley, which indicated that a suspect, or perhaps a third victim, had left the premises. The blood was to the left of bloody, large-sized shoeprints, which indicated a male, possibly injured. The blood trail ended in the alley, where loose change littered the ground, as if it had been spilled when someone pulled keys from their pocket and either didn't notice or didn't have time to pick up the coins.

If the female victim was O. J. Simpson's ex-wife, there would soon be swarms of media and curious civilians. So my first order was to extend the police cordon to the entire 800 block of South Bundy.

Brad Roberts arrived, and I walked him through the crime scene. As I showed him the trail of shoeprints and blood drops, we both saw a bloody fingerprint on the door handle of the rear gate that opened onto the alley. The fingerprint was identifiable, comparable, and high in quality. The fact that it was an impression made in blood meant that whoever left the fingerprint did so after the killings had occurred.

While we were still at the rear gate, Detective Tom Nolan joined us. He also saw the fingerprint.

I wrote in my notes: "REAR GATE, INSIDE BOLT (TURN KNOB TYPE) POSS BLOOD SMUDGE AND VISIBLE FINGERPRINT."

This was a huge lead. If the fingerprint belonged to a victim, then we had a witness. If it belonged to a suspect, we had both a fingerprint and DNA. If the DNA matched one of the victims, we had the suspect's fingerprint in their blood. And if the DNA matched the suspect, that made it much easier to identify him. If his fingerprints weren't in the system, maybe his DNA was.

Both Roberts and I were fairly certain that the fingerprint would identify the suspect. This wasn't crack detective work, just what happens when you walk through a crime scene with your eyes open.

After Roberts and I had finished going through the crime scene, Phillips asked Roberts to interview neighbors who had called the police when they found an Akita dog with bloodstained paws near the scene.

I went inside the condo and sat down on the couch to write up my notes. The notes of the lead detective are among the first and most important documents of a homicide investigation. They are used by the lead detective to record his initial observations and to inventory possible evidence to be photographed and recovered. The notes are read by other detectives and will be introduced as evidence if the case goes to trial, so they must be clear, concise, and well-organized.

After a few minutes, Phillips came into the living room. He told me the case was being reassigned to Robbery-Homicide. This meant it was no longer my case, and I would not be the lead detective. I finished my notes and gave them to Phillips, who put them in a folder he was carrying.

At that moment, I felt both disappointment and relief over losing the case. This was going to be an interesting case, with a lot of evidence and a suspect/victim who had left the scene. But if the female victim really was Nicole Brown, it could turn into a real mess.

———

It was inevitable that Robbery-Homicide would take over. Roberts and I were West LA homicide detectives, and we would not have been able to continue a regular caseload with the addition of a high-profile murder. Robbery-Homicide detectives don't have regular caseloads. They take cases that are complex, logistically challenging, or require coordination with different divisions, jurisdictions, or agencies.

The two detectives assigned to the case were Phil Vannatter and Tom Lange. I didn't know either of them, but I figured they were two competent guys, like the other Robbery-Homicide detectives I had known.

I figured wrong.

Vannatter had not worked a hot crime scene in seven years, a fact he later admitted in the book he wrote with Lange. That lack of experience would show over the next few hours, as both detectives, but particularly Vannatter, made mistakes that even well-trained rookies would have known to avoid. These mistakes would not only seriously compromise the case, but also leave so many clues for the media to find it's incredible that some hotshot young reporter didn't hunt them down and disclose the real reasons the case against Simpson fell apart.

My boss, Ron Phillips, had not done a thorough walk-through of the crime scene like Roberts and I had. I had not briefed Phillips on our observations or my notes. Phillips was a supervisor, not a working detective. This wasn't his case. Yet when Vannatter arrived at the Bundy residence, Phillips chose to brief him on the situation, gave him the folder containing my notes, and walked him through the crime scene. When Lange arrived, Phillips briefed him, too, and led him on a walk-through.

Phillips's decision to show the Robbery-Homicide detectives the crime scene was the first instance I remember of seeing law enforcement professionals disregarding established procedure. I look back and wonder why someone would throw common sense out the window like that. In hindsight, I believe that the blinding spotlight focused on an NFL football giant and movie star was just too bright to resist. Suddenly, police work had gone Hollywood. It was the first of many instances to come in which things were done differently than at any other time in my police career.

It wouldn't be the last.

While Vannatter and Lange worked the Bundy crime scene, Roberts, Phillips, and I went out on the street, waiting for more personnel to arrive so we could be relieved of the case. It was between three and four in the morning, too late to go home, so Roberts and I tried to get Phillips to spring for breakfast before we went back to West LA and started our regular working day.

Then, after less than an hour at the Bundy scene, Vannatter directed Phillips and me to take him and Lange to Simpson's Rockingham estate to make a death notification.

This didn't make any sense. We had not confirmed that the victim was Nicole Brown. We did not yet know the identity of the male victim. And even if we had confirmed the female victim was O. J. Simpson's ex-wife, the lead detectives should never have left a hot crime scene to tell Simpson she was dead.

Keith Bushey, the West Bureau commander, had ordered that Simpson be notified in person, and instructed to pick up his children from West LA Station, where they had been taken from their bedrooms in the Bundy residence. Instead of sending officers with less pressing responsibilities, Vannatter and Lange wanted to make the notification themselves. Strangely enough, they didn't perform the same courtesy for Nicole Brown's family, or Ron Goldman's.

When we arrived at the Rockingham estate, Vannatter, Lange, and Phillips rang the doorbell at the front gate. They waited. And waited. I felt ridiculous standing there with three middle-aged men taking turns ringing the doorbell, so I went for a walk down the street.

I noticed a white Ford Bronco in front of Simpson's house. The vehicle was parked at an odd angle, as if the driver had left it in a hurry. The tires had run into the curb. There was a piece of white painted wood on the parkway, as if it had fallen from the fender, yet no wood resembling that was anywhere nearby. I shined my flashlight on the outside of the Bronco and saw what appeared to be smudges of blood on the door handle. On the car doorsill were marks that also could have been blood. Visible in the rear cargo area were a folded plastic tarp and a shovel, as well as a package bearing O. J. Simpson's name. When I tried to look more closely inside the car, the light from the flashlight reflected back from the tinted windows. It was still dark outside.

I went back to the house and told Vannatter that the Bronco had blood on it. He asked if I was sure it was blood.

"If Fuhrman says it's blood," Phillips said, "it's probably blood."

Vannatter looked perplexed. So I explained that the Rockingham estate might be connected to the Bundy crime scene. Someone walked away from the Bundy scene bleeding. The blood trail ended in the alley behind the Bundy residence. There was blood on the Bronco parked outside Simpson's house. Simpson himself could be a third victim, injured, or possibly already dead.

We didn't have a warrant to enter the premises, but here was a clear case of exigent circumstances—the law allows police warrant-less entry with probable cause. Vannatter didn't seem to understand the concept of exigent circumstances, so I put it in very simple terms.

"We've got to make sure everybody's okay," I said. "We've got to make sure Simpson's not dying in there."

Vannatter agreed. I climbed over the fence and let the other detectives in. Phillips, Vannatter, and Lange knocked on the front door of the residence, but there was no answer. Same with the back door. The first person we found was Kato Kaelin in a bungalow attached to the main house. He told us that Simpson's daughter Arnelle was in the next bungalow. While the others went to find Arnelle, I stayed with Kaelin. Making small talk, I examined a pair of boots near his bed and the shoes in his closet, to see if they resembled the bloody footprints from the Bundy scene. (They did not.)

I asked Kato if he had seen or heard anything suspicious. He said that around 11:00 p.m. the previous night:

"I was just lying on my bed, and there was a big thump on the wall. It made the picture move. I thought it was an earthquake."

Since there hadn't been an earthquake, I figured this might be a clue. So I went outside to look. There was a pathway behind Kaelin's bungalow. I walked down it to see if anyone was still there. That's when I found the bloody glove. It looked shiny and moist. The ground nearby was covered with debris, but none of it had fallen on the glove, which told me it hadn't been there a long time. Further down, spider webs were spread across the path, indicating that whoever had dropped the glove hadn't gone any farther. And it was right near the air-conditioning unit, which that person had probably bumped into, making the noise Kaelin heard.

The glove resembled the one at the Bundy crime scene, which had already been observed by Riske and all the detectives at Bundy, and which I had described in my notes. The resemblance was close enough for me to figure that whoever dropped the glove had come here from Bundy.

Police work is often a process of weaving together known facts with facts you think you know but can't prove yet, to arrive at tentative conclusions, which are either corroborated or contradicted by the evidence as you gather and analyze it. You rarely have absolute certainties—especially this early in a case.

Even though the two gloves were apparently similar in appearance, Vannatter wanted me to return to the Bundy crime scene and look at that glove again.

"I don't think that's necessary," I said. "We've seen both gloves. They're similar type and size. Bundy is a separate crime scene. I could cross-contaminate it."

"I want you to go back there and meet up with a photographer to take pictures of the glove," Vannatter said.

Now I was beginning to worry about Vannatter's competence. But police departments are paramilitary organizations. You can make suggestions, like I did, but in the end, you follow orders. Vannatter ordered me to go back to Bundy. So I went.

At Bundy, I had an LAPD photographer take photos of the glove before I inspected it myself. The glove clearly matched the one that I had found behind Kaelin's bungalow at Rockingham.

Roberts was still at Bundy. Up to that point, no detective had gone as close to the victims as I was ordered by Vannatter to do in order to compare the gloves. When I told him about Vannatter's order, Roberts gave me a look that matched my own reaction. "What was he thinking?"

Roberts and I drove back together to Rockingham. On the way, I gave Roberts an update on the situation there. When we arrived at Simpson's residence, the sun was just coming up.

To me, Rockingham was a crime scene. So I was going to walk Roberts through it. Since my first observation of evidence was the blood on the outside of the Bronco, that's where we started. I showed Roberts the blood and explained how it had been difficult to see inside because of the tinted windows. Roberts cupped his hands around his eyes and looked through the front passenger window.

"There's blood all over the inside," Roberts said. He showed me the bloodstains visible on the steering wheel and center console.

Vannatter was by the main entrance. I called for him to come over. Then I showed him the bloodstains Roberts had discovered.

"Holy shit!" Vannatter exclaimed. He was clearly excited. It was obvious to both Roberts and me that he had not seen this evidence before. Vannatter quickly returned to the house.

Roberts continued to look around the Bronco. He observed drops of blood leading from the driver's side of the vehicle onto the drive-way and all the way to the front door of Simpson's residence. When Roberts reached the front door, Vannatter was standing in the door-way.

"We should probably close off the front door," Roberts said, pointing out blood drops near Vannatter's feet.

"Oh, man!" Vannatter said.

Roberts showed him the rest of the blood trail, leading all the way back to the Bronco.

"That's it," Vannatter shouted. "This is now a crime scene. Let's get everybody out of here!"

Vannatter's sudden decision that Rockingham was a crime scene made it quite obvious to both Roberts and me that he had not seen either the blood inside the Bronco or the blood trail before we showed it to him. Of course, given the lack of light prior to Roberts's arrival, and the fact that we were focused on making sure no one was injured inside the house, it would have been difficult, if not impossible, for anyone to have noticed the blood inside the Bronco before Roberts did.

Meanwhile, the blood trail was in danger of being washed away, because the automatic sprinkler system—usually programmed for early morning—would be going off at any moment. Vannatter and Lange were trying to figure out the computerized control board that ran the sprinkler system when Roberts came over and simply unplugged it. Vannatter didn't seem to appreciate Roberts' common-sense solution.

Vannatter's demeanor at the crime scene made me worry that he was in way over his head. Of course, it was a high-profile murder case, already getting complicated, with two separate crime scenes and a possible celebrity victim or suspect we hadn't yet located. But Vannatter seemed only to be making more mistakes as he went along.

After Vannatter spoke to Kato Kaelin in the kitchen of the main house, he sent Kaelin out into the street by himself. Kaelin's car was there. Nobody was watching him. I didn't want to lose our only witness, so I asked Vannatter what should be done about Kaelin. Vannatter said it wasn't important. I told a patrol officer to take Kaelin to West LA, put him in an interview room and give him a cup of coffee.

Meanwhile, the original crime scene had been left without a case detective while both Vannatter and Lange were at Simpson's residence. Lange returned to Bundy, leaving Vannatter in charge at Rockingham. I later learned that once at Bundy, Lange ordered my original crime-scene perimeter shrunken. This allowed the media to come closer and photograph the female victim. Seeing this, Lange went inside the house and got a blanket to cover her, contaminating the body with possible transfer evidence of hair and fibers. Why would Lange shrink the perimeter? Meanwhile, Vannatter had to go to West LA to write a search warrant for Simpson's residence and get it signed by a judge. So he left me in charge of the Rockingham scene.

The first thing I did was order the Bronco towed and impounded, so we wouldn't risk any evidence being lost, damaged, or compromised. Before he left, Vannatter rescinded that order, saying it wasn't necessary. Later that day, I saw journalists using the hood of the Bronco as a coffee table.

Roberts and I began marking the locations of all the evidence we had observed, in order to preserve and protect it for the criminalists. When criminalist Dennis Fung showed up, he began recovering only some of the blood drops from the driveway.

I thought, this is insanity—why take every third or fourth drop? You take everything. Brad and I looked at other, mentally asking— *what is going on here?*

When Vannatter returned to Rockingham about three hours later, he left the original search warrant on the table in the kitchen. Roberts grabbed it and took it to him.

"You're supposed to leave a copy of the search warrant on the premises," Roberts reminded Vannatter, "not the original."

"Oh," was all Vannatter could say. It seemed like Vannatter did not know a basic police procedure.

Roberts and I both read the warrant and were shocked by how vague, incomplete, and sloppily written it was. We looked at each other and rolled our eyes.

———————

Simpson had been located in Chicago. Once we learned he had left LA around 11:00 the previous night, we began to consider him a possible suspect. He arrived home shortly after noon, while we were just beginning to search his residence.

A patrol officer named Thompson was standing at the Rockingham gate. I had told Thompson not to let anybody enter the crime scene, and if they did, to arrest them. When Simpson arrived, Thompson told him not to come on the property. Simpson didn't stop, so Thompson handcuffed him.

I was inside Simpson's office, watching through the window. Roberts came over and took control of Simpson. They stood beneath a tree by the children's play set. I could see they were talking.

Immediately after his encounter with Simpson, I asked Roberts what was said between them.

"What are you looking for?" Simpson had asked.

"Well, it's not my case," Roberts said, "but we've got a blood trail that goes from the Bronco right up to your house."

"Oh man...Oh man...Oh man..." Simpson said. He broke into a sweat and started hyperventilating.

I told Roberts to write it all down immediately, to note the date and time, and sign the document. This way, if there was a trial, Roberts could support his testimony. We both felt that Simpson's physical reaction to Roberts's mention of the blood trail indicated guilt. If police found a blood trail leading up to the house of an innocent man, it would provoke a lot of questions. Questions like: Whose blood was it? Is anyone hurt? Have you found the killer?

We expected that Roberts's testimony concerning this exchange with Simpson would be an important part of the case. But we were wrong. And, as you will see, the press never followed up on this interaction between Roberts and Simpson either—even though it was broadcast on TV for millions of viewers to see.

Vannatter drove Simpson to LAPD headquarters at Parker Center. His and Lange's interrogation of Simpson proved to be a disaster. The whole point of an interrogation is to get a suspect to commit to a few details, which you can prove or disprove later. You're not looking for a confession, although those are always nice. When they interrogated Simpson, all Vannatter and Lange had to do was get him to state exactly where and when he cut himself, confront him about the blood trail, and establish his alibi, if he had one. Yet, while they asked those questions, they never got clear answers and didn't insist on getting them. They didn't even ask Simpson if he had killed Nicole. The interrogation was so bad that the prosecution never introduced the transcript as evidence (it is reprinted in full in my book, *Murder in Brentwood*), and avoided any mention of it during the trial.

That afternoon, Deputy District Attorney Marcia Clark arrived at the Rockingham scene, saying that she had been called by Vannatter for some advice while writing the search warrant. Now she was on the case.

I had never met Clark before, but her attitude at the crime scene made me uncomfortable. She laughed and flitted around like it was a social gathering and not a homicide investigation. I got the sense that she liked the attention of the television cameras outside and the news helicopters hovering overhead. To me, they were distractions from the work at hand. Worse, they would make a tough job even more difficult.

Roberts walked her through the crime scene. He showed her the evidence discovered: the blood on the interior and exterior of the Bronco, the blood trail leading from the Bronco to Simpson's front door, and the bloody glove behind the bungalow. He also showed Clark a blood smear on the light switch of the maid's bathroom and a pair of black sweats in the washing machine. Roberts explained how he and I had discovered all this evidence.

Later, Clark was joined by Deputy District Attorney Bill Hodgman. Hodgman and Clark sat me down at a patio table by the pool to interview me about our initial observations. In the conversation, I never described any item of evidence being found by Vannatter, because I didn't know of any. Our conversation was often interrupted by the news helicopters just above us. I wondered why we were conducting the interview outside, exposed to the cameras, when it should have been done in the house where we would have some privacy and quiet. And it was unprecedented that District Attorneys (DAs) would come to a crime scene before the evidence had even been collected, interviewing detectives who were in the middle of executing a search warrant. Usually the DAs wait until the detectives put their case together before they talk with them. But TV crews and cameras can be a siren song to DAs with political ambitions. Again, this doesn't make for good police work, or legal process—but it makes great television.

Once we were done being interrupted by District Attorneys, Roberts and I went through the house. Our job was to observe possible items of evidence and bring them to the attention of the Robbery-Homicide detectives who were charged with the collection of evidence. One detective noted where each piece of evidence was and who found it. Another booked the evidence.

You only get one chance to recover evidence. That's why a search should be careful and thorough. The lead detective should do a final walk-through to make sure that no evidence has been missed. If there are any doubts as to whether an item has evidentiary value, it should be recovered, just to be safe.

During the search, Roberts and I observed and called to the attention of the Robbery-Homicide detectives the following pieces of evidence:

- An empty Swiss Army knife box on the edge of the bathtub
- Visible blood evidence in water droplets in the shower and the sink
- Used black terry-cloth towels next to the bathtub
- A blood smear on the light switch in the maid's half bathroom
- Black sweats in the washing machine

In Simpson's bedroom, Roberts found a pair of gloves that apparently matched the gloves found at both crime scenes. When he brought the gloves downstairs to show the Robbery-Homicide detectives in charge of the search, they told him to put them back.

Roberts also observed continuing blood drops from the front door halfway up the stairs to a linen closet. None of this evidence was recovered, including the above list.

Two weeks later, Vannatter got a second warrant hoping to find those very pieces of evidence. By Marcia Clark's own admission later, this warrant was written, not by Vannatter who had sworn to it, but one of the attorneys at the DA's office. The search warrant stated that the pair of gloves Brad had found in the master bedroom had been "inadvertently left behind."

Roberts and I were asked to assist in that second search.

When Roberts read the search warrant, he said, "We already found all this evidence. Why are we going back to find it again?"

But by the time we executed the second search, the house had been thoroughly cleaned, and none of the evidence remained.

On July 5, a preliminary hearing was held to establish if there was enough evidence for charges against Simpson to go to trial. I was not listed as a witness in the proceeding, but around noon I received a call from Marcia Clark. She needed me to testify at 1:30. That was awfully short notice, especially considering Los Angeles traffic. I asked Clark what was going on.

"Vannatter is lost," she said, "he doesn't know how to explain exigent circumstances."

The defense lawyers had filed a motion to suppress all evidence found at Rockingham due to an illegal, warrant-less search. The motion argued that we had entered the Rockingham estate without a warrant, and therefore any evidence recovered subsequently was "fruit of the poison tree," since the search warrant was based on evidence found when we had no legal right to be there.

I drove to the courthouse, eating my lunch of a tuna fish sandwich and apple on the way. When I arrived, Clark was in the hallway outside the courtroom. I could tell she had a problem. She looked very serious.

"Vannatter's losing it on the stand," she said. "You've got to testify."

Clark gave me about three minutes' preparation for my testimony. Then I went into the courtroom.

I had testified hundreds of times, but nothing prepared me for that courtroom. There was a completely different energy. Heads turned when I opened the door. There was a hush of silence as I walked to the witness stand. Most trials are attended by a handful of people. This was a preliminary hearing, yet it was standing room only. There was a television camera and a still photographer in the jury box. I had never before seen a camera in the courtroom. I thought the TV camera was just recording the hearing, but it was being broadcast live. Later, I found out that thirty-two million people were watching.

I sat down in the witness box and did the same thing I had been doing in my eighteen years as a cop. They ask you questions and you answer. You state the facts and don't let yourself get rattled. Just like cops do every day all across this country. Yet I couldn't ignore the cameras trained right on my face.

Gerald Uelmen, a Fourth Amendment specialist from Santa Clara University, represented the defense. He tried to trip me up and bend my words, but we had had really good reasons for entering the Rockingham residence. I explained how exigent circumstances applied to this case. Meanwhile, I was looking at the cameras thinking: *I've got a hole in my pants, where my gun rests on my hip. This is my oldest jacket. I'm dressed to go out in the field and do police work.* Even for an experienced cop, this unprecedented level of media attention was distracting.

After my first day of testimony, I went back to West LA. Brad Roberts had watched the hearing on television. I could tell something was bothering him. When he was angry, he turned quiet. Finally, he said, "Did you forget you had a partner?"

I felt bad because my partner thought I had cut him out. I told Roberts that I hadn't mentioned him because Clark hadn't asked me any questions about anything we had done or seen together. My testimony ran two days, so when I returned to the stand I brought up his name several times, but Clark never pursued those lines of questioning.

I couldn't understand why Clark didn't follow up with questions regarding Roberts's discovery of evidence. She knew of Roberts's involvement in the case. He had walked her through the Rockingham crime scene. Whenever I mentioned Roberts, she should have followed up with a question. Instead, it was almost like someone unplugged my microphone every time I mentioned his name.

Looking back, I also wonder why no journalist was asking: "Where's Fuhrman's partner?" "Why hasn't he been called to the stand?"

Especially with the TV footage of Roberts talking to Simpson and to Clark, any self-respecting reporter should have wondered: "What ever happened to that guy?"

A few days after my testimony, the judge ruled that our entry onto the Rockingham estate and the subsequent search warrant had been legal. All the Rockingham evidence would be allowed.

It's important to understand the difference between a preliminary hearing and the jury trial. In a preliminary hearing, unlike a full trial, one detective can testify to the observations of other detectives, in order to expedite the proceedings.

Sure enough, during the preliminary hearing, Vannatter testified that he had found the blood inside the Bronco and the blood trail leading into the house. Though he was technically allowed to do that if he had been the designated "finder," I felt he should have used Roberts's name and mentioned his role. But worse than that— Vannatter's testimony simply left out a lot of the crucial evidence Roberts had discovered.

As a witness in the case, I had been admonished not to watch any of the proceedings. But Roberts hadn't been admonished. He had seen Vannatter's preliminary hearing testimony and realized that Vannatter was taking too much credit for discovering evidence, describing it inaccurately, and leaving a lot of it out. This was not just insulting— it was dangerous.

CHAPTER NINE

THE WITNESS
EVERYONE "FORGOT"

AFTER MY TESTIMONY IN THE PRELIMINARY HEARING, people began calling West LA to congratulate me. They brought food and cookies to the station. I had a stack of fan mail waiting on my desk every morning. It was nice to get some credit for doing my job, but the attention got old, real quick. The Bureau Chief wanted to have lunch with me. Supervisors and Captains wanted to see me. These are people I couldn't get five minutes with when I was just a working detective. Now that I was a character in a daytime television drama, they all wanted a piece of me.

In every homicide case, there is an interval between the arraignment and the trial. The interval can last four to six months, sometimes longer. During this time, the prosecution and defense prepare their cases. And the detectives go back to work on other cases.

Very quickly it got to the point that I could no longer work effectively on the street. Even when the attention was positive, it made it difficult to do my job. Everybody wanted to talk about the Simpson case, *even suspects I was trying to interrogate*. Anyone I would talk to on the street, no matter what happened, no matter how trivial the conversation, would go to Simpson's lawyers afterwards, looking to cash in. At one court case I participated in, television crews wanted to film my testimony. The judge threw the cameras out of his court.

I was getting all this attention, yet Roberts had done as much, if not more, than I had done in the Simpson case. As I became an overnight household name, he became invisible. He was my partner. He sat right across from me; he saw the gifts and heard the phone calls. And if I couldn't do my job, Brad Roberts couldn't do his, either.

As the weeks went by, Roberts understandably grew more and more angry. Robbery-Homicide often called Phillips and asked him to get Roberts and me to help with the case. We searched empty fields for the murder weapon and interviewed potential witnesses, stuff Vannatter and Lange, as the lead detectives, should have been doing. Phillips's desk was right beside Roberts and me. Whenever Phillips got a call from Robbery-Homicide or the DA's office about the Simpson case, he would talk to me, not Roberts. And Roberts would just stand up, slow and quiet, and get a cup of coffee.

In preparation for the criminal trial, Phillips and I went dozens of times to the war room at the District Attorney's office or Robbery-Homicide Division to discuss the evidence. But after that first day at Rockingham, Roberts was never again interviewed by either the DA's office or the Robbery-Homicide detectives. The DA not interviewing Roberts was bad for the case. But the media not interviewing him was bad for the truth. Both took a back seat to "the show."

After talking to Roberts when she first took the case, Marcia Clark had no further contact with him. The DA's office was interviewing every other police officer who had been remotely involved in the case—patrol officers who had secured the perimeter or canvassed the neighborhood. But nobody was interested in hearing what Brad Roberts had to say, even though *he was the detective who had probably found the most evidence.*

By the middle of August, Roberts was fed up. Though he had done so much in the Simpson case, he had been cut out entirely. He wrote a memo to Deputy District Attorney Bill Hodgman listing the evidence he found and where, and how Vannatter's preliminary hearing testimony was in conflict with the facts. He sealed the letter in an envelope addressed to Hodgman, who was in charge of the case, and asked Phillips to deliver it as he was on his way to the DA's office.

Roberts told me about the memo after he gave it to Phillips. I figured that Phillips would deliver it, Hodgman would read it, then talk to Vannatter and get him to straighten out his testimony during the trial. Vannatter could testify that Roberts found the blood evidence in the bronco and on the driveway at Rockingham. The prosecution could call Roberts to testify to his discoveries. If the defense noticed inconsistencies between Vannatter's preliminary hearing and superior court trial testimonies, he could simply explain that he had testified to Roberts's discoveries as police witnesses often do in preliminary hearings. This would expose him to harsh cross-examination, but it wasn't such a big deal.

The next morning, before Roberts and I had finished our first pot of coffee, Vannatter and Lange showed up at the West LA squad room. There were no niceties, no small talk. They asked Roberts if they could speak with him. He agreed. Vannatter motioned toward an interrogation room, and Roberts and Vannatter went inside.

I figured they were talking about some aspect of the case, like the murder weapon, since it was too soon for any fallout from Brad's letter.

After Vannatter and Lange left, Brad turned to me and said, "Let's get out of here." Roberts and I got in our car. Before we even left the parking lot, Roberts said: "Vannatter had the letter. He said he was the finder, and I had to be ok with that. He said I couldn't testify to the evidence I found."

I was stunned as I slowly realized what had just happened. But then I remembered the key piece of evidence.

"We still have the bloody fingerprint," I said. "Once that's a positive ID, Simpson's going to plead out."

Roberts stared straight ahead, said nothing. He didn't look convinced.

A couple months later, Roberts, Phillips, and I went out to a bar in West LA called the Arsenal. It was a 1950s kind of place with red leather booths. I liked it because they had Patsy Cline on the jukebox. That night we were having a good time, drinking beers and listening to "Crazy," over and over. Suddenly Vannatter showed up. He sat down and ordered a drink. Roberts did not say a word. Finally, Roberts went to the bathroom. As soon as he was out of earshot, Vannatter leaned close to us and asked, "How's our boy doing?"

"Why don't you ask him yourself, Phil?" I said.

But when Roberts came back, Vannatter didn't say anything. He was visibly nervous. The Arsenal wasn't his hangout. We weren't his friends. I can only assume he had come to check up on things; to make sure Roberts was keeping quiet.

Several times Roberts and I talked about Vannatter and whether we should do anything about him, and if so, what. One time we had a very heated discussion in front of Phillips.

"What are you going to do?" Phillips asked. "If you go forward, then we're involved in obstruction of justice."

"We didn't do anything," I said.

"Everybody's exposed," Phillips said.

"We're not exposed," I told him. "What did we do wrong?"

Which made me wonder: was he the one who had given the letter to Vannatter?

––––

When the defense first announced, through an article in the *New Yorker* by Jeffrey Toobin, that they would claim Simpson had been framed by a racist conspiracy orchestrated by me—I didn't even take it seriously. Other people around me did, but I was in a bubble of disbelief. It was so outrageous I simply didn't let it enter my mind. But then, suddenly, I realized they were walling me in, that they were serious. I couldn't defend myself. It was impossible. The whole nation was in a frenzy. As a witness in the upcoming trial, I had been ordered not to follow the case in the press, or to make any public comments. I was one of the few participants in the Simpson case who actually followed that admonishment.

I have already dealt with the allegations against me in detail in my book *Murder In Brentwood*, so I won't take the time to rehash them here. But just try to imagine what it feels like for everyone in the country to be talking about a person you don't recognize—someone who is racist, stupid, evil, and corrupt. And they're calling that person by your name.

When you're a cop, you get used to people attacking you, making bogus accusations of racism or police brutality, and trying to get the crowd to turn against you. Working as a cop isn't a popularity contest.

Some people will hate you no matter what you do. That's part of the job; you learn to live with it. But in the Simpson case, it happened to me with the whole world watching. And I couldn't do anything about it.

Nearly everywhere I went there were news cameras. The defense team hired private investigators from out of state to follow me—and my family. One day a private investigator who had been approached and recruited by the defense to surveil the other detectives and me—not only at our work, but at our residences—came forward and told us what the defense was doing. Did he really feel bad about it, or was it just more intimidation? After that, there was additional security at West LA Station and a LAPD patrol car was parked 24/7 outside my house for some time. Over the years, I have also realized the irony of this media attention on me. While cameras and crews were following my every move, they should have been chasing down the other partner—Brad Roberts—who had not been called as a witness, yet knew exactly what evidence had been discovered indicating O. J.'s guilt.

I kept thinking it would all go away once the case went to trial and Simpson was found guilty. I had never seen a case with so much evidence against the defendant. It was simply unimaginable that he would be acquitted. I wondered why he hadn't already pled guilty.

Then I found out why.

———————

"Don't worry, there's still the fingerprint." That's what I had told Brad after Vannatter had shown up with the letter and silenced him.

But there was no news of the fingerprint, not even in the gossip about evidence you hear leading up to a trial. We figured the prosecution was just waiting for DNA results, since the fingerprint analysis would have been done shortly after Simpson's prints were taken. DNA tests for the trial were being performed by a private laboratory and the Department of Justice. That could take weeks, even months.

In January 1995, as the prosecution made final preparations for the trial, I asked Tom Lange if the fingerprint had come back yet. He didn't say anything. He didn't have to. The look on his face told me something had gone sideways. So, next chance I got, I asked Marcia Clark what had happened to the fingerprint.

She looked surprised and acted as if she didn't know what I was talking about. I told her about the bloody fingerprint that Roberts, Tom Nolan, and I had all seen on the rear gate at Bundy, and I had described in my notes.

"They didn't read your notes."

When Clark said this, I got a queasy feeling in my stomach, like someone had just kicked me in the gut. I had been standing. Then I was sitting down.

"What? They didn't read my notes? For how long?"

"It doesn't make any difference." She replied.

They hadn't read my notes and Clark knew it. They had left the single most important piece of evidence at the Bundy scene. They hadn't even done a thorough walk-through of their own crime scene. (The Brown family had the lock on the gate changed just a few days after the murders, and the locksmith later said that he saw a bloody fingerprint, but thought that the police had already recovered it.)

If they didn't read my notes, what the hell did Vannatter and Lange do at Bundy? The first thing you do when you take over a case is read every single piece of paper in the collection of documents called the "homicide book." In the early stages of an investigation, the crime scene notes, field interviews, and rough sketches are the core of the case, all you have to work with. When Vannatter arrived at Bundy, the "homicide book" was the folder that Phillips gave him, containing only a handful of documents. This is crime scene 101—such standard procedure that it never occurred to me that Vannatter might not have read them or passed them on to Lange, who would be handling the Bundy scene.

I calmed myself down.

Still, I reasoned, even without the fingerprint there was more than enough evidence to convict Simpson. In any normal case, just one drop of the suspect's blood at the murder scene, or one drop of the victim's blood in his car or on his clothing, would bring a conviction. In this case there were some two hundred blood stains, drops, and smudges, every single one of them matching Simpson or one of the two victims and leaving a trail from the murder scene to Simpson's car to his home. Short of a videotape showing Simpson committing the murders, I didn't see how there could have been any more evidence against him.

A few days before I took the stand in March 1995, Clark asked me how I was going to testify if asked about the fingerprint. I said I would describe it as a bloody fingerprint, several points in quality.

"Since you're not a fingerprint expert," Clark said, "you can't say it was a fingerprint for sure, can you?"

"Well, I've got ten," I said. "I've seen hundreds. I've lifted quite a few. I know a fingerprint when I see one."

Besides, I told her, Brad Roberts had seen it, too.

"I don't think we need Roberts," Clark said.

Shortly after that meeting, Vannatter testified in the criminal trial. Once again he took credit for the evidence Roberts had discovered and testified about it inaccurately.

I can't say why he did it. I'm not a judge or a lawyer; I'm a detective. Some might call it bad memory, others perjury. Whatever you call it,

Vannatter saying he found all that evidence did not agree with the facts. And now Vannatter, and the entire prosecution, were stuck with it. If this had been discovered, the truthfulness of his entire testimony could have been called into question. While Vannatter's first search warrant did not specify who initially observed blood inside the Bronco, or the blood trail from the vehicle to Simpson's front door, the defense could have argued that the search warrant had been written and sworn to by a police officer who had lied under oath about the very evidence he cited to justify the search. Very likely, a judge would have ruled for the defense and ordered all the evidence from Rockingham excluded.

On several occasions during the criminal trial, I asked Marcia Clark why she didn't call Roberts as a witness, when his testimony could have helped turn the case around quite dramatically. To take just one example, the defense accused the LAPD of planting a pair of black socks, which contained blood from both Simpson and Nicole, because a video taken by Dennis Fung to memorialize the collection of evidence did not show them on the floor of Simpson's master bedroom. In fact, the socks had been collected as evidence prior to the videotaping. Roberts had initially observed the socks on the floor of the master bedroom early that morning.

Once again, I suggested calling Roberts to testify.

"You can forget about those socks," Clark replied stiffly.

As the trial progressed, it became more and more clear to me that the prosecution categorically needed to call Roberts as a witness. Because of the controversy over alleged racism, my credibility was sinking deeper every day. At one point, I told Clark to simply drop me as a witness. She would lose the bloody glove, but there was still more than enough evidence to convict. Roberts could take my place, and testify to all the evidence that he and I had found.

"You can forget about Roberts," she said.

When Clark made this statement, I realized that keeping Roberts out of the trial was more important to her than anything else. She would rather stick with me as a witness—race card and all—than put Brad Roberts on the stand.

Why didn't Clark bring my partner into the trial? Did she fear that if Roberts were asked about the discovery of blood evidence at Rockingham, he would have revealed that Vannatter had taken credit for finding all the evidence while misstating and omitting key items—and that the entire case could have been in jeopardy? Clark knew he existed—Roberts walked her through the Rockingham crime scene when she first arrived. He showed her the blood inside the Bronco and the blood trail leading up to Simpson's front door. And he described how he had first observed this evidence.

What were Roberts and I going to do? It was a heavy responsibility. The stakes had become enormous. The future of this very important murder case, with the whole nation watching on television, put us in an impossible situation. If we revealed what we knew, the case might be thrown out. We didn't want to be the ones to derail the prosecution. So we kept silent. Our loyalty to the case outweighed our loyalty to the truth.

As the claims of planted evidence and racism accumulated, I kept hoping that some journalist or defense investigator would ask the question: "Where is Fuhrman's partner?" and Roberts would eventually get called as a witness for the defense.

But no one ever asked that question, even though Roberts was featured in the news videos from those first hours of the investigation that the defense was studying like the Zapruder film, hoping to find any shred of evidence that might help get their client acquitted.

Why didn't the defense recognize that such an important witness was missing from the prosecution's case? I think Simpson's lawyers were so focused on stirring up racial controversy that they couldn't see a great opportunity to have the case thrown out when it happened right under their noses. During my cross-examination, F. Lee Bailey sped through questions about my police work and quickly began talking about racism and planted evidence. If Bailey had only asked me the right questions, I would have been forced to contradict Vannatter's testimony. Then Bailey would have found himself in the curious position of having to defend my truthfulness and integrity.

The defense played the race card because Marcia Clark dealt it. In my direct examination, Clark asked me questions about race, opening the door for the defense to question me on cross-examination. If she hadn't asked me about race, I believe it would have been much harder for the defense to introduce it as an issue. Every first year law student knows this. It wasn't about legal competence, but intimidation. Clark didn't want to appear to be avoiding the issue, so she brought it up. The powerful glare of the TV camera lights turned everyone into actors in a sort of soap opera the nation was watching from the comfort of their living rooms.

My direct testimony ended at the point when I returned to Bundy to look at the glove again. Clark never asked me about anything that came afterward, even though I was the detective in charge of Rockingham estate while Vannatter went to write the search warrant.

Of course, if she had asked me about anything beyond that point, I would have mentioned Brad Roberts. My assumption is her questions stopped because she did not want to risk my mentioning Roberts.

I was called back to the stand after tapes of my voice using derogatory language were introduced as evidence by the defense. They had been made to help build characters for a fictional screenplay I was writing with a screenwriter—but that didn't matter to the defense, who was trying to get their client off. Prior to my testimony, I tried to get Marcia Clark to help me figure out some way to reduce the impact of the tapes. As the prosecuting attorney, she could ask me questions in her cross examination that would be tailored to bring out the fact that those tapes were created for a work of fiction. But she wouldn't even talk to me. I honestly don't know if she wanted to distance herself from me because I had become the villain in this drama, or because she was afraid that I might bring up the problems with Vannatter's testimony.

In preparation for my court appearance, my lawyer Darryl Mounger said, "I'm not advising you to take the Fifth."

"If the prosecution would ask me a question where I can clarify my testimony, I won't take the Fifth." I said.

But no one in the DA's office would talk to me. I was completely on my own and left with no choice but to take the Fifth Amendment. I wish they had given me a chance to explain why I had denied using a racial slur. The question F. Lee Bailey had originally asked me was compound and unclear, I took it to mean whether or not I had called anybody the "N" word to their face, where my using it in the writing of a fictional screenplay clearly didn't apply. It was so irrelevant, it didn't even cross my mind when I was testifying. I had completely forgotten it. But O. J. Simpson's criminal trial was no place for me to make these arguments. Certainly not without anyone in my corner.

The defense lawyers knew that once I had taken the Fifth on one question, I would have to respond similarly to any further questions, or waive my privilege against self-incrimination. So after I pled the Fifth, defense attorney Gerald Uelman asked: "Detective Fuhrman, did you plant or manufacture any evidence in this case?" And I had to take the Fifth on that question, too, even though I had not planted or manufactured any evidence. When the question was asked, Marcia didn't object to it. I had put most of my adult life into being a cop; now in an instant, I saw it all destroyed, perhaps because she was still hoping she could win her big case. But the jury came back with the verdict of "not guilty," and Simpson got away with murder.

After the verdict, I was famously blamed for Simpson's acquittal. I can understand why people thought it was my fault, if all they knew about the case was what they saw on television and read in the newspapers.

But Marcia Clark, Phil Vannatter, and Tom Lange also blamed me. And they knew better. I took it on the chin. I could survive that. I kept my mouth shut, not out of loyalty for the case, or the LAPD as a department, or even for the cause of justice. I did it for the cops I worked with, guys I thought deserved my loyalty. I understood I was all alone, and telling what I knew wouldn't have helped anyone. Not even myself. Revealing the truth would only have engulfed my fellow officers in more scandal and payback. There was enough damage done already. I didn't want to inflict any more.

Up until the verdict, I thought Simpson would be convicted. After the verdict, it was too late. Still, a great injustice had been done when

Vannatter could lie about evidence and everybody protected him, while I was charged with perjury for using a racial slur during the writing of a fictional screenplay.

My book *Murder in Brentwood* was released the day after the verdict in the civil trial, where Simpson was found liable for the murders. I didn't appear as a witness in the civil trial, and neither did Brad Roberts, but I was in close contact with the lawyers for the Brown and Goldman families and warned them of problems they might have with Vannatter as a witness. I believe that's why his testimony in the civil trial was limited.

Shortly after *Murder in Brentwood* was published, I submitted to a polygraph examination to finally put to rest the charges that I had planted any evidence in the Simpson case. I passed the polygraph, which included the question: "Did Vannatter find any evidence at Rockingham?" My response was: "No." And the polygraph showed I was telling the truth.

Once again I was leaving clues for someone in the media to pick up on. Yet despite all the attention that my polygraph test received, nobody asked why I had included a question about Vannatter.

In the paperback version of *Murder in Brentwood* I went even further, describing how Brad Roberts had been shut out of the case against O. J. Simpson and pointing out problems with Vannatter's testimony.

Still, nobody made the connection.

———————

Five years after the murders of Nicole Brown and Ron Goldman, I was in Los Angeles on business. I called Bill Hodgman, who should have prosecuted the Simpson case but early on had to leave it to Clark because he had a serious medical condition. I liked Hodgman. He was a tough prosecutor, and straight as an arrow. He had kept in contact with me after the trial, when almost everyone else went out of their way to avoid me.

I told Hodgman I had something very important to tell him, in person. Without asking what it was, he agreed to drive over to Santa Monica and meet with me the next day.

I told him everything—Vannatter's testimony, Roberts's memo, and Clark's refusal to call Roberts as a witness.

Hodgman was upset—I could see it on his face. When I told him about the letter, it was like someone sucked the wind out of his body. He just slumped in the chair, with a look of dread. He said he never saw Roberts's letter, but I already knew that.

"What would have happened if you had received the letter?" I asked.

After a long and thoughtful pause, Hodgman replied, "I'd certainly would have had to interview all the parties involved. And if there weren't satisfactory reasons for what occurred, I'd have to put it before a Grand Jury. And if they chose to indict anyone, that would've been what we had to live with. If they found that there were violations, the case against O. J. Simpson would have most likely been dismissed."

Even considering all this, Hodgman said he wished he had received the letter. Sometime after our meeting, Bill Hodgman called Brad Roberts, who confirmed what I had told him.

On the tenth anniversary of the murders, I appeared on a television special with Geraldo Rivera, in which I revealed that Brad Roberts had written a letter to Bill Hodgman, which Vannatter had intercepted.

When asked about Brad's letter, neither Vannatter nor Lange denied my charges. Here are their verbatim responses.

> "Yeah, ah, I have no comment on Brad," Vannatter said, visibly uncomfortable with the question. "I don't know anything about Brad Roberts. I don't know anything about what he did. So I can't really answer your question. We're talking, we're talking about something that happened ten years ago. A lot of water has gone under the bridge. I had no dealings with Brad Roberts to my knowledge that night or that morning."
>
> Lange said: "Didn't see it. Second time I've heard about it. First time apparently when he wrote it ten years ago. I don't know what was in it. It was alluded to me that he had concerns."

The letter's existence has been corroborated by Lange, Roberts, Phillips, and myself. The fact that Vannatter never even attempts to dispute that it existed is very telling.

I have already taken full responsibility for my testimony in the case and the words I said on the tapes. I apologized in my book and on numerous media appearances. One thing I never apologized for was my police work on the Simpson case. And I never will. If Brad Roberts and I had kept the case, we would have recovered the bloody fingerprint and no doubt matched it to Simpson. End of story.

Instead, Vannatter and Lange took over, to tragic effect.

Shortly after *Murder in Brentwood* was published, Ron Phillips and his wife came to visit me in Sandpoint, Idaho. I wondered why Phillips made the vacation detour to my home. As Phillips and I walked around my small ranch, the conversation eventually turned to the Simpson case. When I mentioned Roberts's letter, Phillips quickly responded, "What letter?"

"Don't try that bullshit with me!" I said, looking him right in the eye. Phillips started hemming and hawing, trying to control the situation. But I saw what my former boss was doing. He was acting just like a suspect. He wanted me to join the conspiracy of silence, so that he could feel better about what happened to me.

The spotlight brings out the worst in people. During twenty years of police work, I thought I had seen my share of arrogance, cowardice, deceit, and betrayal. But that was nothing compared to what I saw in the Simpson trial.

After the Simpson trial, the LAPD Internal Affairs Division, the Los Angeles District Attorney's Office, the California Attorney General's Office, and the U.S. Department of Justice together spent millions of dollars to investigate my police career.

The LAPD Internal Investigations Department had a room that measured six hundred square feet, filled with cardboard boxes stacked six feet high. That room contained every single scrap of paper from my twenty years on the force. They scrutinized every case I ever worked, investigated every partner I ever had.

None of these investigations found any wrongdoing whatsoever. That didn't surprise me. What did surprise me was that not one single investigator ever talked to me. If you're investigating a possible crime, don't you talk to the suspect?

Maybe they didn't want to hear what I had to say.

Cops live in the real world, so that civilians can live secure in their fantasy that the world is a safe and peaceful place. Civilians turn off the lights and lock their doors and go to bed. That's when the real world comes out to play. In this game, there are good guys and bad guys. All night, they go at it. Sometimes the good guys win. Sometimes the bad guys get away.

And when the sun comes up, the civilians walk outside and get their newspapers and it's a fresh, clean world, because cops have cleaned up the mess and taken out the garbage.

That's what makes it great to be a cop. We're protecting people who don't even realize it. We're making communities safer. Every violent criminal we get off the street, every gun we take away, stops a crime—even saves a life. When we're really successful is when stuff doesn't happen. Nobody notices. And that's okay. Because we know.

As tough as the real world can be, at least the rules are clear. In the Simpson case, the rules were like Wonderland. In many ways, the Simpson trial was the first "reality" crime show. But it wasn't real at all. It was complete fantasy.

Millions of people watched the Simpson trial. They thought they were learning about law enforcement. Instead they were just projecting their own feelings onto the characters they saw. Whether it's love or hate, pride or disgust, fear, envy, whatever—people want to see their emotions played out on a grand stage. Briefly, I was the hero. Then I became the villain. I didn't want to be either. I was just a cop trying to do my job. Yet that simple effort unleashed a hurricane of consequences for my family and me.

Fame is indelible. It's like I'm always wearing a t-shirt that says in big bold letters, "You Know Me." But the public doesn't know me. They know an image they have created in their own minds, for their own reasons. Maybe I have been able to change that image a little, but I am still stuck inside it, like a bad costume I did not choose but can't get out of, like Halloween 365 days a year. "Mark Fuhrman," is not who I really am. It never was. I am not the only one who experienced having his life, name, identity, sense of self, and everything else turned inside out and upside down by the Simpson trial. It happened to all of us, on both sides.

But sometimes I do wish I could go back. Since I was a kid, growing up in a less than idyllic childhood, to be sure—all I ever wanted to be was a cop.

For all my flaws and failures, I sincerely believed in my job. I was fair and loyal to my partners. I considered their lives my responsibility. For twenty years I had their backs and they had mine. I never sacrificed another cop to cover up my mistakes. I never let a good cop take the fall for someone else. I stayed loyal to my fellow officers, whether they deserved my loyalty or not—even when my own reputation was at stake.

FOX has given me back the capacity to do investigative work on homicide cases, and I am very grateful for that. Now, fourteen years later, as part of the media, I have an even greater perspective on how off-center the coverage of the O. J. Simpson case was. Bottom line: The media missed the boat. They forgot how to be journalists because they were too busy entertaining people.

Even after the trial was over, their job wasn't done. Was there no more investigative reporting left to be done after the Warren Commission "closed the book" on the Kennedy assassination? Follow-up investigation was needed—and I was counting on it.

I expected a young journalist to pick up on the clues in my testimony and in interviews years later and to start chasing people down. It should have been painfully obvious to any investigative reporter that the whole story was not being told every time I mentioned Roberts's name on the stand. Where were the watchdogs in pursuit of truth, not ratings?

We are now witnessing the death of print newspapers. Will that mean even less investigative journalism than we have now? Where will we get our news if cable networks are satisfied recycling rumors as facts and dropping phony updates every hour instead of chasing down the real story? Crime as entertainment has become so intoxicating, it's very difficult to go back. But all it takes is one person—one journalist willing to step outside the circle and investigate the facts. One Woodward or one Bernstein could change the entire industry, remind reporters of their responsibility to the public, and balance out the soap opera on the air. Then—and only then—could Americans once again rely on the *news*.

INDEX